# Since 1969, hundred and businesses have benefitted from Karl Bareither's FBR System℠

**Now you, as an advisor, can learn how to better serve your family business clients.**

**Here's what business advisors say:**

"Karl, I want to thank you for speaking to the Yuba Sutter Estate Planning Council. I believe that your remarks were well received and of real benefit to the participants. I was particularly impressed by the questions from attorneys who indicated that they had struggled with the very issues that you were discussing."

— John L. Guth, Attorney, Certified Specialist in Estate Planning

"Thank you Karl for speaking at our National Conference. Your presentation definitely touched the hearts of our advisors."

— S. M., Advanced Markets Consultant

"Karl spoke at our Farmers Tax and Accounting Conference and he received excellent ratings. I was very pleased with his presentation and would recommend him as a speaker."

— Kay Phelan, Director of Conferences
California CPA Education Foundation

"I learned a structure to approaching the business owner: technical plus communication both important."

— T. S., Financial Advisor

"The FBR System approach will cause a serious re-thinking of my role."

— L. G., Planner

**Also by Karl Bariether:**

Planning a Family & Business Legacy
*A holistic approach to wealth transfer planning for entrepreneurs, business owners and family members*

# Becoming a Wealth Transfer Specialist

### A proven holistic model for financial, tax and legal advisors to expand their family business practice

## Karl Bareither, CLU
### Wealth Transfer Specialist

#### with

## Tom Reischl, CLU, ChFC, MSFS

**Important Note:**

This publication is intended to provide accurate and authoritative information with regard to the subject matter covered. It is offered with the understanding that neither the publisher nor the author is engaged in rendering legal, tax, financial or other professional services. If legal, tax, financial or other expert assistance is required, the services of a competent professional should be sought.

The authors and publisher specifically disclaim any responsibility for any liability, loss or risk, personal or otherwise, which is incurred as a consequence, directly or indirectly, of the use and application of the contents of this book.

Published by FBR Publishing
P. O. Box 2347
Avila Beach, CA 93424-2347

Cover design copyright © 2003 by Cameron Clark

Copyright © 2003 by Karl Bareither

ISBN 0-9727716-0-3

Printed in the United States of America

The publisher offers discounts on this book when ordered in quantity for bulk purchases and special sales. Please contact FBR Publishing, 805-595-2089 or *info@fbrsystem.com*.

# Contents

# Dedication

While in Australia some years ago, a trade association group asked me to write a "how to" book documenting my 30 years experience helping business-owning families transfer their wealth to succeeding generations. They wanted to be able to help association members' tax, financial and legal advisors learn how to move beyond traditional wealth transfer planning and become Wealth Transfer Specialists.

At the time, I thought this would be a relatively easy task, lasting perhaps a few months—certainly not more than a year. Eight years later, I have finally concluded recording my work experiences with the help of many individuals and groups. It seems that just a simple thank you is inadequate for the ideas, encouragement and advice so many have shared with me.

However, there are two people I want to especially recognize for their assistance. Tom Reischl, more than any other person, is responsible for assisting me in writing this book. I'm not sure it would have been completed without his help. In addition to his writing talent, he is truly a delightful person to work with. The other key person is Lillian, my partner for 49 years, who was willing to make many sacrifices over the last several years and encouraged me in so many ways. Without her help, I could not have finished this project. Thank you both!

More than two hundred family business owners, their family members and trusted advisors, have provided me with their various perspective during the past thirty years. This has resulted in my defining the client as the entire family and recognizing that open family communication is essential to a healthy family and business life. They also helped me realize the value of moving beyond transaction orientation to a process planning approach and establishing greater client objectivity by employing wealth transfer planning fees. Many other individuals have assisted me—and you know who you are! I thank all of you for providing input to help me better serve my family business clients—and in some cases, teaching me what not to do.

This book is dedicated to the many business owners, family members, professional advisors, friends and trade associations who have made it possible.

After reading this book, I trust you will consider learning to become a Wealth Transfer Specialist yourself, building upon this model for helping family businesses minimize the role of the IRS, enhance the quality of family life, and increase business profitability. You will find the quality of your own life enhanced as well.

# About the Author

Karl Bareither is founder and president of FBR System, Inc., a family business wealth transfer planning firm, and teaches advisors how to use a holistic process approach to transfer wealth and renew both business and family. He teaches numerous workshops and training courses in this unique family-based approach to wealth transfer planning, and has authored the book *Planning a Family & Business Legacy*.

Bareither holds degrees in business and communication from Northern State University, South Dakota. He graduated from Purdue University's Estate Planning Program and has earned the Chartered Life Underwriter (CLU) designation. He has been a successful financial advisor and served as training director and regional sales director for a major financial services company. Bareither has been involved in many professional organizations including several estate planning councils, AALU and The Family Firm Institute. He is a Qualifying and Life Member of the Million Dollar Round Table. He has also been admitted to the Top of the Table.

Bareither is an instrument-rated pilot with a multi-engine rating, enjoys reading, studies Eastern philosophy with Western eyes, plays tennis, and travels in his motor home. He and his wife, Lillian, reside in California. They are parents of three children and grandparents of four.

# Preface

If you are currently actively working in the family business market, you probably spend all or most of your energy serving the business owner. The typical business advisor treats the business owner as the only client and confines the fact-finding process to discovering what the owner needs and wants. The business owner, too, generally believes decisions affecting the business are his alone to make. I believe there is a better approach.

## The Family as Client

In my work with family businesses, I engage the entire family, not just the business owner, as the client. From the outset, I obtain agreement from the business owner that every adult family member's expectations and goals are considered in order for the owner to make a more informed decision. My objective is to create a plan for the preservation and transfer of the family's entire wealth, not just the business. In order to do that, it's necessary to create a plan that will reflect the needs, desires and expectations of the entire family. Contrast this approach with the typical business advisor who deals only with the business owner and focuses exclusively on the owner's desires.

To develop the information needed, it is important to personally interview every member of the family, including spouses. Frequently everyone in the family does not necessarily share the same objectives for the business as the owner, and the only way to understand what the various attitudes are is to ask. It is important to interview every family member in a "safe" setting where they can be comfortable sharing open, honest answers to the open-ended questions posed. I ask about family relationships, communication problems affecting family members, and probe expectations related to the future of the business and their perceived role in it. Gathering opinions from the owner's other trusted business advisors is equally essential. The information obtained helps me understand the objectives of the family regarding the transfer of the family's wealth.

Once the information is obtained, I work with other trusted advisors of the family to develop a new wealth transfer plan. I use computer software I have developed for this purpose. The software creates a report that describes the current wealth transfer plan and makes recommendations for the necessary changes to meet the objectives. The report is written in layman's language so everyone in the family can easily identify concerns and solutions.

## The Family Retreat

The new plan is then presented to the entire family at a family retreat. The retreat is conducted at a neutral site, where there will be no distractions. Every adult family member and their spouse is invited and expected to attend.

The retreat experience is always meaningful. Many business owners I've worked with have told me that this was the first time they ever heard their children speak openly about the business and their expectations. Often, the children's comments trigger deep emotions in themselves and others. Sometimes conflicts arise. These are important to address because conflict and hidden agendas can jeopardize the success of the business, quality of family life, and the wealth transfer plan.

In many cases, the family retreat is the first time the family has ever openly discussed business and financial matters. I call my process "family and business renewal" because, while it helps preserve the business and other family wealth, it also enhances family relationships by opening the door to better interfamily communication.

## Compensation

You may be wondering how I can afford to invest so much time and energy on each case. Well, the answer is simple. I charge a fee for my wealth transfer planning. My clients believe my services provide considerable value. The fee typically ranges from $10,000 to $40,000, depending upon the size and complexity of the case. I have received over $1.5 million in wealth transfer planning fees from my practice. I guarantee to refund the entire fee if the client family is not completely satisfied with my work, eliminating their risk. I find business owners are not reluctant to pay my fee once they understand the nature and scope of the work I plan to do for them.

You can experience similar success in the family business market by following these basic principles: treat the entire family as your client; consider the family's entire wealth, not just the business; focus on a process, not merely transactions; present the new wealth transfer plan in a retreat setting; charge a planning fee for your services.

# Introduction

If you currently make your living advising family business owners, you already know that it is a fascinating field of endeavor. Working with family businesses offers exciting opportunities to be of service and be well rewarded in the process. Part of the attraction in working with family-owned businesses is the fascinating interplay of personal, tax, financial, legal and business matters. The family business advisor has to be part technician, part salesperson, part planner and part communication expert in order to be effective. Business succession planning and estate planning is not as straightforward as some might think.

Consider this true story:

Fred, a California business owner client, came to this country as an immigrant, and over 30 years had built a multi-million dollar business empire. His son, Ralph, attended some of the best higher educational institutions and had many of the attributes necessary to run the family business. In some areas, Ralph was even better qualified than his father. Nevertheless, Fred was uncomfortable with Ralph taking over the business because he felt his son lacked humility. The father felt the son had always "had it made" and had never suffered or done without, and therefore, lacked empathy for the employees of the business. The difference between the values of the two generations was massive. And a generation gap like this is often at the root of family miscommunication—in and out of the business.

The reality is that while the need to blend the personal and the business is easy to observe, it is rarely taken fully into account by advisors who work with family owned businesses. That's where this book comes in.

Traditionally, family business owner advisors have stuck to their particular discipline—be it taxes, insurance, financial or legal advice—and rarely ventured into attempting to understand the whole picture of both family and business. Most advisors see the business owner as the "client" and do everything they can to understand that individual's needs and satisfy those needs with advice and services tailored to the owner alone. Isn't it strange then, that so many family businesses fail to survive beyond one or two generations? If the advice is tailored to suit the business owner, why does the plan so often fail? If the business owner is surrounded by technical experts and knowledgeable advisors, why doesn't the family business continue to benefit succeeding generations? Where's the disconnect?

The problem is most family business advisors concentrate on the owner and business to the exclusion of the family. However, in the end, it's the family dynamics that ultimately control the future of the business. Meeting the business owner's needs is only a partial solution. In order to assure the successful transfer of the family's personal and business wealth, the family must be involved; and family issues—however emotional or controversial—must be addressed.

This book is a road map for a process that will take you from being a traditional family business advisor to becoming a Wealth Transfer Specialist. The benefits are many. Helping a business owning family deal with difficult communication issues can be very rewarding personally. I treasure the letters I've received from family members expressing their appreciation for my help. Here's a typical example.

*"We want you to know how appreciative we are of the work you have done for our family business. When you started wading through all of the issues and dealing with all of the family members, we could not have imagined that we would be able to resolve some of the difficulties that existed. This*

*would not have been possible if you had not taken the personal interest in our business and in our family that you did."*

—A. M.

Not only is there the personal satisfaction of knowing that your solutions will indeed preserve the family and the business for generations to come, but the financial rewards are considerable as well. You're about to learn how to supplement the income you currently receive by working with family businesses and receiving wealth transfer planning fees for work that few are doing. This differentiator will set you apart from your competition and create opportunities you never imagined.

Changing your focus from the business owner to the family is the key to increasing your personal satisfaction with your work and increasing your personal income. Also, moving from a transaction to a process relationship will provide opportunities to increase services and establish greater client trust and loyalty. This book will show you how to do it. I know this model works because I have personally built a successful fee-based family business practice using these principles. It can work for you!

*Karl Bareither, CLU*
*Wealth Transfer Specialist*
*President and Founder, FBR System, Inc.*

# Chapter 1

## My Journey from Advisor to Wealth Transfer Specialist

*Let him that would move the world, first move himself.*

—*Socrates*

The land my family currently lives on is part of what was once a nine-thousand acre ranch, perched above the shimmering California coastline. A successful ranching operation, owned by a single family since 1882, was lost after a 20-year legal battle that tore both family and ranch apart. Had the family been able to successfully plan for its continuation, cattle might still be grazing on the spot occupied by our house. You might say our home is testimony to the consequences of lack of communication between the owners and heirs of a family business.

Not far away, another family feuding over a business resulted in land baron Clarence Salyer losing control of his empire when two of his sons rebelled and forced him out of power. To this day, the family is still split into two irreconcilable factions. About the only time the remaining Salyers get together now is for periodic courtroom sessions.

The case of the Fairview Dairy is yet another example of a failed business transfer plan. (Note: all of the following examples are based on real cases, but names have been changed to protect confidentiality.)

Fairview Dairy is a successful dairy farm owned and operated by Peter, a first generation American who came to this country as an immigrant with no formal education and no capital assets, save his willingness to work hard. Over time, Peter's hard work and excellent management skills resulted in his developing a high-producing, quality milk operation. After many years, he built up a multi-million dollar dairy business. As he got older, Peter decided to bring his son, Tony, into the business with the goal of eventually passing the business on to him. Unfortunately, Tony had other ambitions.

In a private meeting with Tony and his wife, Patty, I learned that their interests were quite different from Peter's. Their dream was to start a small dairy operation of their own in another state. Although Peter couldn't understand why Tony didn't share his vision of keeping the dairy in the family and building even greater production and profitability, he nevertheless helped Tony start his dream operation by giving him enough cows to get started. Tony and Patty moved to another state and began building their dream dairy operation.

The point of this story is that the vision of the second generation may not match that of the entrepreneur when it comes to the future direction of the business. It's important that this be understood in order to avoid a lot of pain down the road. The only way that can happen is if there is open, honest communication among family members when it comes to dealing with matters of the family business.

Having worked with business owners for years as an active financial planner, I dealt with many cases like Fairview Dairy. Businesses that could have—perhaps should have—survived to enrich new generations of family owners, but instead, were liquidated or sold to others outside the family.

Why is it that only 30 percent of family-owned businesses make it to the second generation? What goes wrong? I think I know the answer.

## Getting Started

I started in the insurance business in 1958 working my way through college by selling life insurance. Hours of study to learn about the products my company offered were in addition to my regular student workload. It took a lot of practice to learn how to make effective presentations. Countless phone calls and door knocks searching for people to tell my story to. Perseverance eventually paid off; and within a couple of years, I began to experience a fair amount of success.

Success was an opiate to me. A taste of it bred a desire for more. By 1961, I was a full-fledged workaholic. The life insurance business, in those days, presented no limits on the individual willing to pay the price for success—and I was willing.

My hard work paid off. Success brought with it many perks, including a life style many would envy. A beautiful home, airplane, houseboat, and a show horse. Creature comforts. Financial security. All the trappings of a successful, hard-working entrepreneur.

Along the way, I discovered a knack for sorting through complicated situations and developing creative solutions. I gravitated toward more complicated cases such as estate planning and small business succession planning. As time passed, I found myself most attracted to working with small- to medium-sized business owners and their families.

I followed the usual path in developing my skills in advanced marketing. My workaholic nature drove me to pursue additional education in estate planning and business planning. In 1972, I received the Chartered Life Underwriter (CLU) designation.

By 1978, I had settled into a comfortable work style that included conducting financial seminars sponsored by third-party trade associations and banks. Taking advantage of my strength as a technician, I managed to build a very nice, stable clientele base. Clients became friends in the process of helping them plan for the continued success of their businesses, adding to the personal satisfaction I received from my work. The financial rewards continued to pour in. In almost every respect, I had it made. All respects, but one, that is.

## The Shoemaker's Children

One feature of my work that always mystified me was the fact that, while the solutions proposed to my business clients were virtually always technically correct, they didn't always solve the problem. Sometimes my ideas worked and sometimes they didn't. The fault didn't seem to lie in the solutions themselves—there was something else happening. Something not clear to me until a crisis occurred in my own family.

In 1986 my only daughter, Karla, died. Not by accident or sickness, but by her own hand. My wife, Lillian, and I were devastated. I had no idea Karla was experiencing major depression. I was too busy to see. In classic workaholic fashion, while busy helping other families with their needs, I had neglected many of the needs of my own family. The shoemaker's family had been going barefoot.

In hindsight, there were signs. One day, not long before she died at age 24, Karla approached me and asked if I would agree to seek outside help and attempt to bring our family of five closer together. Karla knew something I didn't know. While we were obviously prosperous, something was missing. The relationship between Karla, her two brothers, her mother and me was not as close as it might have been. Communication was not as open as it could have been. Karla desperately wanted us to be a closer family; one where each was willing to listen to the others' needs; one where the father had time—quality time—to spend with the family. But while Karla was pleading for me to take time to smell the flowers, the workaholic in me was admonishing her to plant flowers.

To placate Karla, Lillian and I agreed to seek outside help if she could convince her two brothers to participate. We knew Karla would not be successful in convincing her brothers. Frank communication in an open, family gathering environment was simply not our style. I didn't believe it was going to happen—and it didn't.

Eventually, Karla gave up trying to convene the family meeting, and then one day she just gave up everything.

No amount of time, no words, no degree of counseling can ever completely erase the pain of losing our daughter. There is simply no way to rationalize away the fact that Karla found life unbearable—unlivable. Our family relationship may not have been entirely at fault, but I can't help but think I could have been able to do something to prevent her death. Perhaps if the lines of communication had been more open between us, she could have let the family know of her pain, and we could have intervened with professional help. The unanswered questions and feelings of guilt experienced after a loved one commits suicide are the heaviest burdens you can imagine.

If any good can come from such an awful experience, I like to think it's that I learned something from Karla. I learned the value of family love and the importance of open communication among family members. The value of taking time to smell the flowers after working to plant them. The bitter cost of yielding to the temptation to measure one's worth only in terms of work and accomplishments. Our family can never heal our relationship with Karla, it's too late for that. But the four of us can honor her by working to improve our relationship with each other and by extending the lessons we've learned to other parts of our lives.

## Finding Peace of Mind

Given my propensity to overwork, it would have been easy for me to deal with my grief by burying myself even deeper in my work. But that would have required my ignoring Karla's wishes yet again. Instead, I chose to alter my work habits and search for balance between work and family, and at the same time, bring the lessons I learned about the importance of family relationships into my work.

I began to see my work with family businesses in a new way. I began to realize that it wasn't only about technical solutions, after all. It wasn't about finding the most tax-favored way to pass the family business or the most effective estate planning technique—it was about the family itself! I emerged from my grief with a mission: to find a way to literally put family ahead of business.

I hired a firm to conduct a survey of my clients and verified what I had begun to suspect. In many family-owned businesses, a serious breakdown in family communication hindered both quality family relationships and business profitability!

It was during this time that a family asked me to interview all their family members in order to help them prepare a new plan that would meet the needs of all family members. One of the children lived a long distance from the rest of the family and was not actively involved in the business. The family felt it was important to plan for the future of the business while the matriarch was still living and in good health.

Eventually, the planning process resulted in a plan whereby the inactive child was to receive non-business assets instead of a minority interest in the family business. Everyone in the family was satisfied with the results of the planning process. Active family members would own the business, and the inactive family member would receive non-business assets.

Armed with this success, I committed myself to finding a new way to work with family businesses. Instead of working solely with the business owner, I would work with the entire family. Instead of agreeing to develop an owner wealth transfer plan in secret, I would encourage openness on the part of the owner and all family members. Instead of focusing only on the technical aspects of the planning solution, I would search for ways to renew the quality of life for both the business owner and the family members.

Over a period of years, applying these new principles to my work with families and their businesses, a cohesive process with a beginning, middle and end, eventually began to emerge. A process that ultimately leads to a plan for the business that meets the needs of all family members—not just the business owner. A process that also met my own need to apply the lessons Karla taught me and spread the word that having a successful business and a successful family life are not mutually exclusive goals. With this book, I hope to be able to spread that word!

## A New Way of Working with Family and Business

Over time, this work has led me to develop a model called Family & Business Renewal (hereafter referred to as the Model). I like to think that my personal evolution was from a general advisor to a specialist. From a technician—using my mind to match problems and solutions—to an artist, if you will, working from the heart to conceive, design and build something new. Over time, the Family & Business Renewal Model has developed into a truly unique way of doing business. More like building a monument to a family or entrepreneur than simply closing a sale. I began to see myself not as a sales person or simply an advisor, but rather a wealth transfer "architect." The more I thought about it, the better I liked the concept. Karl Bareither, Wealth Transfer Specialist.

The Model begins with the recognition that the client is the entire family, not only the business owner. This in itself was a revolutionary breakthrough in my own thinking about clients. I had always felt that whomever paid my bill was the client. No longer! I'm convinced that business planning cannot be done in a vacuum. Regardless of who pays, it is the whole family that matters. An example will illustrate the importance of family relationships in business planning.

I'm reminded of Arnie, a successful grape producer client of mine. I was enjoying a conversation in the vineyard one day with Arnie's son, Milt. Normally a pleasant, amiable fellow, Milt's demeanor suddenly changed mid-way through our conversation. It took me a minute to realize what had provoked this sudden change in Milt's personality. It seems Arnie was approaching us, and the sight of his father had instantly turned Milt's attitude from positive to negative.

The reason was obvious to me. Arnie had always exercised a great deal of control over Milt, never letting the young man forget who had the power and control—in the family, as well as in the business. Although Milt was heir apparent of the family's business, Arnie had never treated him as anything other than a glorified "go-fer." Arnie's need for power and control over his son prevented him from recognizing his son's potential as a businessman. Arnie refused to invest in Milt by grooming him to be his successor and developing Milt's skills and expertise. Over the years, Milt grew resentful of this treatment, and while he continued to work in the business, his relationship with his father steadily deteriorated. Needless to say, the tension between father and son also prevented any serious planning for business continuation.

Clearly, this is a case where ineffective communication between family members was at the root of the planning problem—and no amount of sophisticated technical training was going to solve it! The family relationship sickness had to be addressed before effective planning could begin. To try to develop and implement a business solution in the midst of the family distrust, hidden anger and hurt would be futile indeed.

As we work our way through the Family & Business Renewal Model, several important principles will be repeatedly emphasized:

- Work with the family, not just the business owner
- Open the agenda to include everyone in the family
- Recognize the most important business asset—the people
- Create a climate for open dialog and communication
- Design a workable solution
- Implement the plan and follow up

These principles and others were developed over time as I gained experience working with families, deepening my commitment to renewing both families and their businesses. The business I created was formed for the express purpose of developing and implementing new ideas for business transfer planning. I chose a motto that I believe says it all: *Preserving the past…Protecting the future…Starting now!*

I've also begun to train others to use the Family & Business Renewal Model and develop their own skills in working with closely held businesses and the families who create them, operate them, and live day-to-day with the challenges they pose. In this book you will learn step-by-step how you can use the Family & Business Renewal Model in your practice to help your business-owner clients plan for the distribution of their wealth and the future of their business. And, in the process, start your own personal journey from advisor to specialist.

Advisors working together

# Chapter 2

## The Challenge

*From the same materials one man builds palaces, another hovels; one warehouses, another villas; bricks and mortar are mortar and bricks until the architect can make them something else.*

*—Thomas Carlyle*

If you've been involved for a while in helping families plan for the disposition of their business at death or retirement, you've probably noticed the same phenomenon I have. Sometimes the plan you develop for a client works and sometimes it doesn't—even though the technical aspects of the plan design are fine. Why is that? Why is it that in one case a particular business continuation plan works perfectly and in the next case, with similar characteristics, the same plan fails?

The answer lies not in the plan—the plan design is not the problem. Usually there are a number of different alternatives that can accomplish the objectives. There is almost always more than one way to solve a problem. After developing a plan based on all the information needed, the trick is to get the plan implemented—therein lies the challenge.

## Focus on the Business Owner

If you are like most successful small business advisors, you probably focus your attention on the "owner" of the business, typically the entrepreneur who founded it. Indeed, if you are an attorney working with small businesses, you may feel an ethical obligation to work with only the business owner. Some legal experts feel that an attorney can represent only one person in a family, and the concept of including other family members in the business planning process represents a conflict of interest. Other legal experts, however, believe it is ethical to work with multiple family members because the "business is the client." Attorneys practicing in the family business market must consider the ethical implications of working with multiple family members and determine whether a waiver is needed.

Although we generally refer to them as "family businesses," often a small business is really an enterprise owned by an entrepreneur. It becomes truly a "family business" when other family members enter the business as employees or managers, or when the entrepreneur dies or retires and ownership passes to the next generation. Two or three siblings owning and operating a business enterprise pose an entirely different set of problems and challenges for the advisor than a sole proprietorship. Cousins as business owners present yet another set of challenges. Still, planning advisors tend to want to identify the sole owner or the majority owner as the client or "customer," seek to learn what the owner wants and then develop a plan according to his or her wishes. To understand how this approach can backfire, it's instructive to examine how such an arrangement might play out.

In some families, the business owner dictates all the decisions, both business and family. In these cases, you will usually find a great deal of family conflict. The owner often wants to maintain a position of power and does so by employing hands-on control and secrecy.

I remember one case where this was followed to the extreme. Pete was a very successful retailer and wholesaler, and he had a son, Jerry who also worked in the business. Pete had very little confidence in Jerry, however, and never permitted him to get involved in the management or operation of the business. Pete died at the ripe old age of 85. Jerry, who was age 65 at the time, had never been permitted to make an important business decision and had no idea how to manage the business. Within six years, the bank owned the business. How long could your business perpetuate itself if your heir is no more than a "go-fer" for the parent?

In many cases, this type of business owner doesn't consult with any other family members while planning for the transfer of the business either. Indeed, from the business owner's perspective, there is no need to consult with other family members ("It's my business, so I make the decisions"). As a result, the business succession plan is often conceived and implemented in secret—if at all. It often becomes known only when the business owner dies, and the plan is finally revealed. Perhaps a simple will has been drafted, instructing that all assets be divided equally among the children. The owner feels this is being fair. ("How can I be criticized for treating all my children equally?") In reality, owners could make more informed decisions if they were aware of the children's goals.

From the perspective of the children, however, while technically equal, this arrangement seems anything but fair. Children who have spent years working in the business may feel they deserve a larger share or control of the business. Non-business children may prefer cash or some other asset rather than being tied to a business operated by a sibling.

Let me tell you a real life story about just such a situation.

The Lazy J is a second-generation Wyoming cattle ranch. I first met Jake, the 56-year-old son of the founder, at the conclusion of a business wealth transfer planning seminar I presented to a group of business owners, sponsored jointly by several banks. Jake was one of five children in the family and the only one working in the family business. His brothers and sisters were all well educated and working in professional or highly-skilled occupations. Jake and his wife Martha lived and worked on the ranch with Jake's parents, Mel and Alice, for thirty years. Jake and Martha always assumed that someday, somehow the ranch would be theirs. Whenever Jake asked his father about the future of the ranch, he was always assured that indeed, someday the ranch would be his.

When Mel died, Jake learned that all the ranch property had been owned jointly by Mel and Alice, and that Alice was now sole owner. Jake wasn't concerned, however. He was certain that his mother would arrange to leave the ranch to him at her death. When Alice died, however, her will provided that ownership of the ranch was to be divided equally among her five children. Instead of becoming successor owner, Jake had merely a one-fifth-minority interest in the Lazy J. To add insult to injury, Jake had always worked for low wages—considering it an investment in his future—and the ranch had never installed a retirement plan of any kind. Jake and Martha had very little to show for their thirty-year investment.

The tragedy of this story is that the failure to plan had destroyed the opportunity for the one person with the most interest and experience in running the family business to take it over. Jake couldn't afford to buy out his siblings, so the ranch had to be sold. A business continuation plan could have been constructed that would have left the ranch to Jake, and other property or assets, such as life insurance proceeds, to the non-ranch children. The business could have remained in the family for another generation—and maybe many more! The problem wasn't the lack of a plan—they had a plan. Apparently the plan was for Mel to leave the ranch to Alice, and Alice's plan was to leave it equally to the kids.

The problem was lack of communication! A plan could have been developed with input from all family members. With an open agenda, Martha's concerns about equal treatment for all the children would have been addressed. Jake's dream of someday owning the ranch might have been considered. The non-ranch children's lack of interest in the ranch could have been taken into account. The technical solution would have been a piece of cake for any knowledgeable advisor—but the family dynamics precluded such a solution ever being developed.

Jake told me this story with tears in his eyes. "Who can you trust if you can't trust your own father?" he asked. "I hope you can help others avoid the same fate."

In the final analysis, the only really effective way for an advisor to develop a wealth transfer plan that meets the diverse needs of all the family members, as well as those of the business owner, is to treat the entire family as the client. This may cause some discomfort for the business owner who is not inclined to be open about business planning, but it's the only way to assure the continuation of the business (assuming that remains the ultimate goal) while treating all family members fairly.

To understand how damaging secrecy can be when planning for the future, consider these real life case responses from one family member who was interviewed about the future of the family's business.

*What is your major concern about the business?*

I want to know when, how and to whom the business will be transferred. There is too much secrecy about the business partnership. I never see the financial statements of the business. I don't know if I will be treated fairly.

*How do these concerns affect you and other family members?*

I'm concerned about stress within the family and the business. I've developed high blood pressure as a result.

*In what areas do you feel the family communicates effectively?*

None—other than socially. There's a lot of anger and coded messages. Alcohol is a problem.

*In what areas does the family communicate poorly?*

Anything to do with money. Decision making is difficult—it's always very non-emotional. Some family members see themselves as victims. Some have poor attitudes and are jealous of other family members. There's very little caring communication.

*Are you in favor of the business continuing?*

Yes, but only if it stays profitable. Changes need to be made. I need to know what is going on.

*What would you like to see happen?*

We need a third party to determine the economic value of the business. I think some of the real estate should be sold and a trust established.

*Do the family members work together productively?*

Only in a crisis. The brothers don't work well together. Someone has to deal with their big egos.

*What additional information would be important for me to understand?*

My family never includes me. I don't feel close to my family. Alcohol is a problem. We never have business meetings. I don't feel I want to be partners with my family in this business.

Imagine, with feelings like these lurking just beneath the surface, how difficult it would be to develop a meaningful plan for the continuation of this business by talking only to the business owner!

As you can see from the dialog above, failing to gather input from other family members when developing a plan for the continuation of a business can lead to failure—regardless of the technical merits of the plan.

## Making the Effort

I think of business wealth transfer planning as a process. However, the typical transaction-oriented sales person might see the process like this:

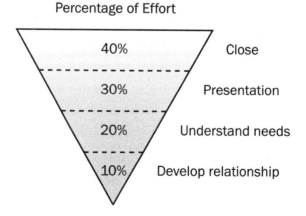

### Traditional Transaction Approach
Percentage of Effort

40% — Close

30% — Presentation

20% — Understand needs

10% — Develop relationship

Most of the time and effort is spent making the presentation and trying to close the product sale rather than trying to get to know the family members and discover their individual and collective needs.

I suggest this practice is upside down. Ideally, it should look like this:

## FBR Process Planning Approach

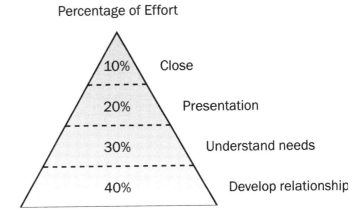

The wise advisor will invest most of his or her time and energy in developing the relationship. That means taking time to get to know not only the business owner, but also all the family members and their spouses—those involved in the day-to-day operation of the business and those not directly involved. The time spent up front building a trusting relationship will lay the groundwork for the development of a business continuation and wealth transfer plan that is not only technically sound, but also has a high likelihood of success. Not only successful from the business perspective, but also successful in promoting a quality family life.

Investing time building relationships also minimizes the effort necessary to close the sale. Once a new plan is developed that takes into account the needs of all the stakeholders, not just the business owner, the solution practically sells itself! When the need is clear to everyone and the solution makes sense, there is little or no resistance to implementing the plan. Problems arise when the solution is based on the advisor's understanding of only the owner's needs, rather than the entire family's needs. That's when time and effort must be spent convincing the family stakeholders in order to close the sale!

## Charging Wealth Transfer Planning Fees

Obviously, discovering all the family's needs can be a time-consuming procedure. And how is the sales person compensated for the time spent if the best solution doesn't require a product from the advisor's portfolio? Part of the solution is for the advisor who wants to be successful working with family businesses to change the way he or she thinks about selling solutions. The typical product sales person is paid by commission only, which often becomes the driving factor in the traditional transaction approach. As a result, impartiality is frequently lost and credibility suffers. The sales person's objectivity may be questioned because the owner and the other advisors know the sales person does not get paid unless something is sold.

I submit that the truly impartial advisor adds value to the process by bringing a certain level of expertise to the table. Expertise in tax, legal considerations and financial products is part of it, of course, but expertise in dealing with people—sometimes difficult people—skillfully persuading them to avoid procrastination and take action also adds considerable value. A competent advisor is entitled to be paid for this added value. This expertise can be rewarded financially by charging a fee—I call it a value-added planning fee.

Early in my career, I relied upon product commissions for my entire income. In many cases, I detected a feeling on the part of my clients, their advisors and prospects that my advice was "tainted" by the need on my part to make a sale. A friend of mine suggested that I set myself apart by charging a planning fee for my work rather than just depending upon product sales.

This change was a difficult one for me even though I had been investing a great amount of time in the planning practice. The first time I provided a prospective client with a proposal for fee-based service was a real learning experience. When my client asked me what the cost would be, I was somewhat hesitant to respond out of fear for what his reaction would be. I finally quoted a total fee of $500. He told me he was surprised that my fee would be so low! I didn't tell him that prior to this quote I was giving my services at no cost other than expecting clients to purchase a life insurance policy from me.

The experience helped me change my attitude toward charging a fee for my services. After all, the owner's tax and legal advisors were all charging fees for their expertise, why wasn't I? Did I think my contribution to the planning process had no value other than when I sold an insurance policy? Besides, there were many times when the owner was uninsurable or resisted purchasing my products for one reason or another. In those cases I was working for nothing. Was my advice only valuable when I was able to sell an insurance policy? I decided it was not.

Eventually I became comfortable with the notion of charging for my services. The lesson I learned from my first fee-for-service client helped me raise my sights. My fees increased over time to the point where it often exceeds $30,000 for a complex case. (See the appendix for a sample client planning fee agreement.)

Charging a fee has another benefit. When the advisor positions himself as a fee-for-service Wealth Transfer Specialist, rather than a traditional product salesperson, the advisor/client relationship changes. Knowing that the wealth transfer specialist is being compensated by a fee eliminates many of the concerns the owner and other family members might otherwise have about the objectivity of the advice they receive.

I believe that it's time financial services professionals stop measuring their value only in terms of product sales made. A very wise person once told me "Only the lead dog in a dog sled team ever gets a change of scenery." If your goal is to change your own personal scenery, to become more than a commissioned product seller, "bean counter" or legal draftsman, you'll have to move up to the lead dog position. That means getting out of your personal comfort zone and working to master new process skills and techniques. Take heart, however. You wouldn't be in this business, reading this book, if you weren't a "people person." Your existing people skills are the very ones you'll need to develop and refine in order to become the consummate family and business advisor—a Wealth Transfer

Specialist (hereafter referred to as the Specialist). It merely takes commitment on your part and a bit of hard work and skill development.

I earlier described my own evolution from advisor to a wealth transfer specialist. To make your journey successful will require change, but making the transition to a Wealth Transfer Specialist leads to many rewards—financial as well as emotional. It's very rewarding personally to be able to help families work their way through often very difficult terrain and emerge renewed. Not only in their business relationships, although that is certainly a driving factor, but also in the improved quality of their family relationships. Resolving long-held grudges and dealing with deeply felt hurts and fears breathes fresh air into all aspects of the family relationship. At the end of the Family and Business Renewal Model, not only is the business healthier, but so is the family!

## Losing the Sale, but Winning the Peace

There's another reason to charge a value-added planning fee for your work. Sometimes the best solution for everyone concerned doesn't include a product sale.

One case in particular comes to mind when thinking about resolving the business needs without selling a product.

My clients, John and Martha, owned a large and successful dairy operation that they operated with the help of their two sons-in-law. One was in charge of the farming unit, and the other was responsible for the dairy operation. Each son-in-law owned 20 percent of the business; John and Martha owned the remaining 60 percent. To my surprise, the individual interviews revealed that both sons-in-law were unhappy in the business and secretly wanted out so they could start their own businesses.

The two men did not get along and their relationship had been strained for most of the 15 years they worked together. During family celebrations and get-togethers, the two men would sit on the same side of the table, but at opposite ends of the table so they would not have to talk or even look at each other. John would spend much of his workday acting as go-between trying to keep the peace between his sons-in-law. Martha once told me she could tell how things had gone during the day by how frequently John turned over in bed that night.

In-depth separate interviews revealed that one of the families wanted to move to another state and buy a smaller dairy. The other family wanted to stay in the area with John and Martha, but operate their own, much smaller dairy. Eventually, both couples did just that. Each family owning and operating their own business finally brought peace to the family.

John and Martha hired a non-family general manager, a key person, to help operate their business. After adjusting to the initial disappointment, they became much more content than they were previously. Under the new arrangement, all the stress caused by the family infighting was eliminated from their lives. Without the need to constantly referee family tensions, they finally had time to travel and enjoy themselves. John and Martha are satisfied with their new life and are considering plans to retire and sell the business to another dairy family.

When this case began to develop, there was no hint it would end up as it did. A straightforward business continuation plan, developed without full knowledge of all the facts, would probably have included a typical buy-sell arrangement to ensure the continuation of the business. That plan would probably have been doomed from the start, given the animosity between the two future owners. What would life be like for John and Martha had they attempted to tie the future of the family and the business together using a traditional business continuation plan?

This was clearly a case where the best solution was no sale! But I still got paid. In fact, my compensation was two-fold: the value-added planning fee I received for working through the procedure and the personal satisfaction I got from seeing this family rid itself of the relational poison that had been plaguing it for years.

## A Proven Way to Lead

We began this chapter by discussing the stereotype of the hard-driving entrepreneur and the challenges presented when it comes time to consider giving up control of the business. Concentrating on the needs of the entrepreneur is one model for the advisor to follow. A second model is to consider the entire family as the client and look for solutions based on everyone's needs. In the preceding chapter I shared the personal experiences that led me to develop this new model for working with family businesses. I've since spent fifteen years proving that the concept works.

The final Model took some time to develop. At first, I attempted to meet with the entire family as a group to determine their needs. I quickly found out that because of family dynamics and underlying tensions, many family members did not feel safe or comfortable sharing thoughts and feelings openly in front of the entire family. In addition, some family members were not comfortable sharing the family's "dirty linen" in front of a relative stranger. The process improved dramatically when I began to interview family members individually, in a private setting.

The key was to meet individually with family members (and spouses when applicable), to learn in detail about their hopes, dreams and expectations regarding the family business. I assured each one of confidentiality in order to encourage as much openness as possible. Later, when it came time to discuss needs and solutions with the family as a group, I used all the appropriate information I had gathered, but did so with anonymity. All the feelings and concerns were aired, but without the personalities attached to them.

It was like the parting of the Red Sea!

I find that in the proper setting, the family as a group is usually genuinely interested in exploring all of the business and family issues raised by the individual members. The group meeting, or family retreat as I like to call it, provides a sense of openness that encourages family members to respond with empathy to the concerns uncovered by the individual interviews. Each family member feels they are being treated fairly because they see their concerns placed on the table and addressed openly by the family. In return, they feel more inclined to consider concerns raised by others objectively. The open airing of concerns, hopes and needs acts as a catharsis for the family. In many cases, the family retreat experience is the first time the family has ever openly discussed many of these issues!

Think of it! In so many cases, when the business is poised at a critical fork in the road—literally developing a map for its future—much of the most critical information needed to make intelligent decisions is hidden from view or buried under layers of stubborn silence and resentment. Is it any wonder that so many business continuation plans fail? The wonder is that any of them succeed!

Preparing to lead the Family and Business Renewal Model is not as daunting as it may seem. Again, you probably already have many of the skills, abilities and knowledge you'll need. They simply need refinement. We'll examine the role of the wealth transfer specialist and the attributes you need to be successful in that role in the next chapter.

## A Success Story

Lest you think that every family business is owned and operated by a dysfunctional family, let me relate a case that was the direct opposite.

John and Nancy were the owners of a very successful cattle ranch in California and the parents of 7 sons. Although the early years were rough, the family worked hard and ultimately built a very successful business in partnership with John's brother and sister.

When I first met John and Nancy and their family, I was struck by the atmosphere of love and mutual respect the family members had for one another. No infighting. No animosity. No communication problems. Although family dynamics was not an issue for them, John and Nancy still wanted to work through the Model in order to structure a fair settlement for their children and minimize tax consequences.

This was an awesome family to be involved with, and it was a real pleasure working through the method with them. The result of the planning was to reorganize John and Nancy's one-third interest in the business into a Family Limited Partnership (FLP). John, Nancy and the seven boys were all owners of the FLP with future growth in the value of the business accruing to the boys. The fact that the family all got along so well together made the multiple ownership of the FLP a feasible option.

As it turned out, none of the boys ultimately became active in the business, and the decision was made recently to sell out the family's interest. Because of the structure of the plan, the boys now own the largest share of the value of the business interest. The final result of the sale is that each family member will walk away from the business with his share of the value in cash. And, being minority owners, John and Nancy will be taxed at a lower rate than they might otherwise have been—meaning they will get to enjoy a larger share of their proceeds from the sale.

Passing the business to the next generation is not always the best solution—as this case proves. Sometimes the best solution for everyone is to sell the business and divide the proceeds. In this case, the functional family dynamics made it easy to provide a fair, reasonable solution that benefited everyone concerned—a happy ending for a happy family.

## Chapter 2 summary points:

**In this chapter we discussed:**

◈ **Most business advisors consider the business owner the client and only take into account the owner's needs and desires when assisting with business planning.**

◈ **The FBR method treats the entire family as the client and works to discover the needs and desires of all family members, including in-laws.**

◈ **Many advisors expend little of their energy on relationship building because their focus is only on the business owner. The most time and energy is reserved for attempting to close the sale.**

◈ **The FBR Process calls for expending the most time and energy on building relationships with the entire family. As a result, the close is almost automatic, requiring far less effort.**

◈ **The key to success in working with family owned businesses is to charge a planning fee for the added value the FBR Model brings to the table.**

# Chapter 3

## The Wealth Transfer Specialist

*Every man is the architect of his own fortune.*

*—Sallust*

Anyone who makes their living working with people's finances—be that providing tax advice; selling insurance, investments or banking products; or designing trusts and other legal documents—knows that the single biggest obstacle to success is the human being's natural tendency to procrastinate. No matter how compelling the presentation, the single most frequent response heard by the professional is, "I want to think it over." Indeed, a large part of what the advisor is really paid for is the ability to persuade prospects to take action. This seemingly simple task is much more difficult than many people imagine.

When dealing with issues around family wealth transfer planning and the continued life of a business, the task of persuading individuals to act becomes even more vexing. This is due to the complex mix of family and business needs and the involvement of multiple personalities.

### The Goal of the Wealth Transfer Specialist

Although the basic objective of all small business advisors is to persuade the members of a family business to take some form of action, the Wealth

Transfer Specialist's purpose must include something additional. To be an effective Specialist, your purpose must be to reform and renew both family and business.

Think of it in terms of how you might explain your intentions to a potential client. What do you suppose the reaction would be if you said something like this?

> *"I'm here to try to persuade you to buy some products from me that will help keep your business in the family."*

Kind of gets you right here, doesn't it?

If your sincere purpose is to preserve the family's wealth and protect the future of the business for the benefit of the owners and their families, as well as employees and their families, why not come right out and say so? You'd get an entirely different reaction. For example, what if you said to a prospective client:

> *"I see myself as a resource. I can help you review the options you have for protecting your business and preserving your other assets."*

You probably wouldn't use the first approach, but the problem is that you might not use the second one either. Why not? What's wrong with openly stating your intentions to a potential client? If you were a prospect, wouldn't you appreciate an open, honest approach by a concerned advisor?

It's a matter of having a noble purpose, which is always very easy to disclose openly to a potential client. If your purpose is less than noble, you're reduced to finding clever words and tricky phrases to disguise your motives rather than being able to honestly state your true purpose. Think about that.

## Skills of the Wealth Transfer Specialist

You accomplish business and family renewal by understanding the human dynamics present in every family and business situation, as well as the nuts and bolts of wealth transfer planning. The only way to become skilled at this is to develop your own level of knowledge and skill. The nuts and bolts part is relatively easy. It's a matter of studying the tax, financial and legal considerations around estate and business transfer planning. You are very likely doing a fair amount of that already.

Building skills in the area of interacting with people, sometimes very difficult people, is something else again. No doubt you already have a considerable degree of skill in this area as it relates to one-on-one or one-on-two meetings—that's probably your typical scenario when dealing with financial products and other kinds of transaction services. Most other advisors of closely-held businesses follow this same pattern—they tailor their presentation for the business owner and perhaps the business owner's spouse. In some cases (group insurance or retirement plan sales, for example) advisors also might make presentations to groups of employees—another very valuable skill you may have already developed.

In order to renew both family and business, however, an additional skill must be developed—something more akin to a mediator or group facilitator's skill. To be effective as a Specialist, the advisor must be able to win the trust of an entire family, uncover all the facts or opinions (including those that are sometimes difficult or controversial), use this information to develop a new plan for the future that meets the needs of everyone involved, and then convince the family to implement the new plan now. Sound difficult? It can be.

Let me give you an example of a case that could have benefited from mediation. This family was split over a non-business issue that was very important to the owner.

Edward and Mary had a very successful cattle operation. They had three children, two boys and a girl, Nancy. As the children grew older, the boys joined their father in the operation of the ranch. Nancy began dating a young man, James, who happened to be of a different religion. Edward couldn't accept James because of his religion and insisted that Nancy not go through with wedding plans. He told Nancy that if she went through with the wedding, he would exclude her from the family inheritance. After much soul-searching, Nancy decided to marry James after all. The result was that Edward cut off all contact with his daughter and never again had anything to do with her or her family.

In every sense of the word, Edward was a successful business owner. However, his need for power and control over his daughter destroyed an otherwise beautiful father/daughter relationship. This case is an example of how a family dispute, stemming in this case from the control needs of the business owner, affected the plans for the future of the business. Mediation may have helped Edward see the unreasonableness of his bias against James. Unfortunately, his prejudices got in the way, so we'll never know if Nancy or James might have been able to contribute to the long-term success of the business. Of course, the effect on the family in this case, is even more tragic!

## Interpersonal and Communication Skills

To be successful as a Specialist, certain interpersonal skill, or personality traits, if you prefer, must be well developed.

### Problem solving

First of all, there has to be a sincere desire to help people solve problems. A large part of the wealth transfer challenge is to work out solutions to complex problems. Not only technical problems, but problems stemming from poor communication between various family members, as well. If your primary objective is to sell one of your products, you'll possibly arrive at a completely different solution than if your motivation is really to develop the best solution for everyone. As we discussed in the last chapter, sometimes the best solution may not include a product sale at all!

### Active Listening

Hand in hand with the desire to solve problems is developing open communication skills. The most critical communication skill is active listening. This means listening not only with the brain engaged, but with the heart as well. Effective listening skills includes being non-judgmental and remaining objective. Again, it starts with a sincere interest in doing what's best for the client—that's the whole family now, remember, not just the business owner! Entire books have been written on listening skills and techniques. Find a good one and study it—you can't know too much or get too much practice listening. Many people believe that an advisor gets paid for talking. I submit that effective advisors get paid for active listening.

### Data gathering

Sincere interest in your clients and effective communication skills come together in a big way during the fact-finding or data gathering. The key here is to ask a lot of open-ended, probing questions. You'll find examples of these in the sample fact-finder contained in the appendix. Ask every question of each family member and pay close attention to his or her responses. Always remember there are no prizes for successfully filling in the blanks of a fact-finder. The fact-finder is only a tool; it's your understanding of the individual family member's needs that's important. Use the fact-finder as a guide for your interviews, but don't let it become a crutch or an end in itself. Strive to gather all the relevant information from each family member about their hopes and dreams for themselves, their families and the business.

It helps a lot if you enjoy the data-gathering procedure. Look at it as an interesting challenge and the opportunity to get to know people in a very intimate way. I find that during the data-gathering process I sometimes learn more about an individual than even their closest friend knows. I often smile to myself on the way to a data-gathering interview because I know I'm in for an interesting couple of hours, and at the end of the interview I'll have made a good friend out of someone who may have previously been a stranger. Such is the power of the skillful interviewer sincerely interested in understanding the interviewee's point of view rather than pushing his or her own agenda.

Did I mention you should also come to the interview prepared to enjoy the experience? Data gathering doesn't have to be a dry, Dragnet-style interrogation ("just the facts, Ma'am"). Help people relax during the interview with appropriate humor and by repeatedly demonstrating your sincere interest in them. Do this by asking them about themselves and then listening carefully to their responses. You pay a huge compliment to a person by listening to them and then writing down what you heard. When was the last time someone took the time to listen intently to you and even went so far as to take notes about what you said (psychotherapists and court reporters excluded)? The data-gathering process is powerful and has the potential to create a bond, enhancing trust between you and the client.

### Verbal Communication

Assuming you have good listening and fact-gathering skills, your next challenge is verbal communication. A critical communication skill for the wealth transfer specialist is the ability to convey complicated information and concepts in a clear, concise manner. If you've ever experienced a client saying to you, "For the first time, I think I understand my trust document (or insurance policy, portfolio, etc.)," you know how rewarding this particular skill can be. Being able to convey complicated topics in a way that a client can understand is a real talent that can be developed with practice.

A good way to test yourself is to ask a member of your own family or a friend, someone without an advisor background, to role-play a proposal with you. After you've made your presentation, ask them to explain it back to you in their own words. If they understand it well enough to be able to do that, you've done a good job of communicating.

### Group presentations

Lastly, being able to communicate effectively in group settings is a vital skill for the wealth transfer specialist. Remember that you'll be making your solution presentation to the entire family in a group setting. Many professionals have anxiety about making group presentations—and perhaps some that don't have any anxiety should. This is definitely one skill that only comes with practice. You simply cannot build group presentation skills by reading about them—you have to do it. It's like learning to fly a plane. How would you feel the next time you board a plane if the pilot announced before take-off, "Ladies and gentlemen, I've never actually flown one of these 747s before, but I've read quite a bit about them. Let's see if we can get this baby off the ground!"

One of the best ways to practice group presentation skills is to get involved in the leadership of a service club like Kiwanis or Jaycees where there are plenty of opportunities for you to speak before groups. Making presentations to service clubs as the featured speaker is another excellent way to gain group speaking experience. In addition, the exposure will serve you well. The absolute best way to master public speaking, however, is to join your local Toastmasters club. You'll be poised and confident in front of groups in no time!

## Practical Skills of a Wealth Transfer Specialist

In addition to the interpersonal skills described above, there are a number of practical skills a Specialist must have or acquire.

### *Conflict management*

The previous chapter contained excerpts from an actual interview with a family member. Some of the concerns that surfaced during that brief discussion dealt with some pretty serious family relationship issues. Problems and issues like alcohol and drug abuse are not unheard of among families who own a business. As a wealth transfer specialist, you'll encounter everything from total family bliss to highly dysfunctional families—and everything in between. Conflicts do occur, and you have to be able to recognize, understand and manage them.

The story in the previous chapter about the two sons-in-law that couldn't stand to be in the same room together is a case in point. The truth is that in many cases a strong-willed entrepreneur can be difficult to deal with—especially for other family members. Past history may suggest that any disagreement with the entrepreneur results in an argument. As a result, family members who fear conflict avoid it by not openly disagreeing. Important topics that might be controversial are shelved for later—but later never seems to come. The resulting buried anger and resentment is sometimes expressed in unexpected ways—often unrelated to the real concern.

Another common cause of family conflict is the inability to distinguish between the family life and the business life. Often the lines are blurred because the family has never taken the time to establish family harmony, nor has a clear business objective ever been established. Instead, family problems seep into business relationships, and business problems find their way into family disputes and disagreements. It's not uncommon to hear "I work harder than he does, but we both get the same pay!" from siblings working in the family business.

The Specialist must be able to identify underlying conflicts within the business and the family and effectively deal with them. To ignore conflicts as the process unfolds is to doom the solution before it's even developed. Keep in mind, however, that you are not a counselor or family therapist. If serious issues exist between family members, it may be best to recommend a professional counselor to help the family deal with them.

### Facilitation and mediation

Another closely related skill is that of facilitating group discussions and mediating differences during the family retreat.

Facilitating discussions between family members is more than simply making a group presentation. In fact, it's the most difficult aspect of the Family and Business Renewal Model. It calls for "thinking on your feet" and dealing with the unexpected. It means having an organized agenda for meetings and sticking to it. It's dealing with conflicts and secret agendas by encouraging family members to share them openly and honestly with each other and then helping find constructive ways to deal with them.

This particular skill is especially important during the family retreat when you are presenting the new plan to the assembled family. The retreat must accomplish its goal of resolving disagreements and conflicts to everyone's satisfaction and gaining support for the new wealth transfer plan. Chapter 6 contains a step-by-step walk-through of the process and outlines various tools and techniques for managing the family retreat and mediating any conflicts that arise.

## Business Knowledge and Expertise

Finally, you won't be surprised to learn that the Specialist must have a considerable degree of knowledge and experience in the area of business and estate planning, as well as knowledge of products, tax laws and a host of other financial matters. Some of these important issues will be discussed later, but detailed information regarding these subjects is beyond the scope of this book.

Every business advisor, of course, must recognize the importance of keeping up to date on tax laws and other legislation affecting small businesses and their owners. Pursuing recognized designations, such as CFP, CLU, ChFC, LLM and CPA, is an excellent method for keeping technical skills sharp. If you haven't already done so, add other professional designations to your list of personal goals. Professional designations rank you with those who truly are interested in their chosen profession and willing to invest in themselves. Remember that you will be working with other professionals with designations who have high expectations of the business advisory team.

In this chapter, I've described in general terms the role of the Wealth Transfer Specialist. In the next segment we'll begin studying the Family and Business Renewal Model itself in more detail.

# Chapter 3 summary points:

In this chapter we discussed:

◈ The role of the Wealth Transfer Specialist

Facilitator

Mediator

Advisor

◈ The skills necessary to be an effective Wealth Transfer Specialist

Facilitation skills

Mediation skills

Interpersonal and communication skills

Business knowledge and expertise

# The FBR Model
## 3 Phases, 9 Steps and 3 Benefits

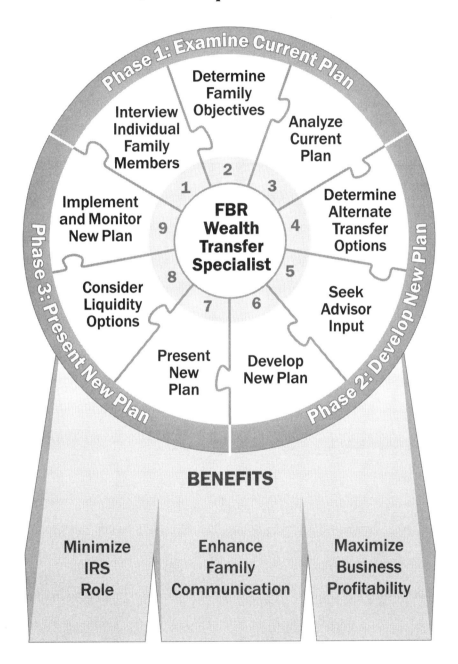

**Phase 1: Examine Current Plan**

Determine Family Objectives

Interview Individual Family Members

Analyze Current Plan

Implement and Monitor New Plan

Determine Alternate Transfer Options

**FBR Wealth Transfer Specialist**

Consider Liquidity Options

Seek Advisor Input

Present New Plan

Develop New Plan

1 2 3 4 5 6 7 8 9

**Phase 3: Present New Plan**

**Phase 2: Develop New Plan**

**BENEFITS**

Minimize IRS Role

Enhance Family Communication

Maximize Business Profitability

# Chapter 4

## Phase I: Understand Current Plan and Family Objectives

*We will never be able to make a machine that will ask questions. The ability to ask the right question is more than half the battle of finding the answer.*

—*Thomas J. Watson*

In this chapter we begin to examine the three phases and nine steps of the FBR Wealth Transfer Model. The Model consists of three phases, each with three distinct steps to follow. The overriding objective is to realize the following three benefits: minimize the role of the IRS in the family's business, enhance family relationships to improve the quality of family life and maximize the profitability of the business.

This graphic on the preceding page best illustrates the Model. Note that the three phases form the outside of the circle, breaking it into three equal segments. Each segment is further broken down into three distinct steps. The completed circle rests on a foundation of the three benefits just discussed. We will return to the diagram from time to time to track our progress.

The Model begins with forming a complete understanding of the current business transfer plan. The objective is twofold: understanding the existing family wealth transfer plan; and developing an understanding of the wants, needs and desires of family members so that this information can be used to craft a new plan.

The process for understanding the existing wealth transfer plan consists of interviewing individual family members, key non-family employees and trusted family advisors, and examining any and all personal and business documents. Typical documents you must gather include:

- Wills and trusts
- Business agreements
- Life insurance policies
- Balance sheets (personal and business)
- Profit and loss statements
- Tax returns for last two years (personal and business)
- List of family advisors (attorney, accountant, financial, etc.)

More will be said later about the information that must be collected in order to develop a new family wealth transfer plan. There are two objectives here; understanding the current plan and understanding the family's objectives. The goal of the individual interviews is to gather all the pertinent information pertaining to the existing plan and the development of the new plan. For clarity, we'll address these two goals separately.

## Step 1: Interview Individual Family Members

The first step in the Model is to uncover each individual's needs, desires and expectations with regard to the future of the business by personally interviewing each family member and spouse.

This frequently is the most fascinating aspect of the whole Model. It's also the point where all the advisor's communication skills get a real workout. As we discussed in the previous chapter, effective listening, probing questions and accurate note taking are absolute requirements for this assignment.

As alluded to earlier, this aspect of family member interviews almost certainly will uncover areas where the family culture mixes into the business culture. Jealousies and family rivalries may surface in response to probing questions. Again, a trusting relationship and the promise and expectation of confidentiality are critical to this process.

The appendix contains a sample of the fact-finder used to guide the individual family member interviews. Let's review the questions and consider the information they might elicit.

*"Describe your major concerns regarding the business."*

*"How do these affect you and other family members, now and in the future?"*

These two open-ended questions are intended to uncover the concerns, reservations and fears the family member might have about the business and his or her role in it. These questions invite a discussion about the current state of the business and can provide insight into existing problems.

Depending upon the responses to these questions, be prepared to probe further into exactly what is causing each concern. The answers to the second question should not be limited to affects on the business. Concerns about the business that affect family member's personal lives are important to note. Remember that the goal is renewing both business and family. Problems in family communication are certain to affect the business relationships and ultimately the wealth transfer planning.

*"In what areas does your family communicate effectively?"*

*"In what areas does your family communicate poorly?"*

It's always wise to pose positively worded questions before negative questions, if at all possible. Even the most dysfunctional family communicates well in some areas. Here's a chance to recognize the positive aspects of family communication. Who knows? You might be pleasantly surprised to learn the family communicates very well in many areas including the business. If true, that would certainly be important to know—but don't hold your breath!

The answer to the second question, of course, is to try to zero in on areas of communication in which the individual feels there are problems. Again, be prepared to probe deeper depending upon responses.

If the interviewee is reluctant to respond to these questions, you might generate participation by revealing information from prior interviews—but be careful here. To betray the confidence of another family member will destroy your credibility. You might say something like "It's my understanding there is concern that the owner avoids discussions involving money. Would you agree with that?" Don't use comments from other family members if they include hints about who may have said it.

> *"Over what issues and between which individuals do you experience communication breakdown?"*

This question zeroes in on the relationship issue. The individual being interviewed may experience difficulties communicating with one or more individuals in the family or business. If communication difficulties exist between the current owner or owners and the future owners, this will seriously impact the wealth transfer planning. Be on the lookout for communication triangles. Son, for example, has difficulty communicating with father, so he enlists mother to act as a go-between. Mother, in this scenario, becomes caught up in all sorts of game playing and may end up choosing a side—making the communication rift even deeper.

Another thing to watch for is spontaneous corroboration of communication difficulties. For example, if son indicates he has difficulty communicating with daughter, and later, father indicates that son and daughter have difficulty communicating, it's probably true. Corroboration is valuable as it adds certainty to the diagnosis of communication difficulties.

*"Are you in favor of the business continuing in this or another form?"*

*"If not, what would you like to see happen?"*

These questions can elicit some very important information. It's possible that the heir apparent of the family business doesn't want to continue it. Or, she may want to continue it without the other family members— but has never been able to convince her parents of that fact or is reluctant to state his position because of fear of the reaction. Any number of other important opinions might come to light as a result of questions and subsequent probing. Perhaps the next generation owners secretly want to break the business into more than one unit and operate them independently from one another.

In any case, if there is a desire on the part of any family member to do something other than continue the business in its present form, it's very important for you to know, as that could significantly impact the business transfer plan.

*"Do you think your family members work together productively?"*

*"What are your suggestions for improving productivity?"*

These questions, like the questions about communication, invite each family member to comment on the dynamics of the family at work. They may also bring out dissatisfaction with control issues. This line of questioning might also lead to recommendations related to personal development of one or more of the future business leaders. In a nutshell, the more you can learn about how the family relates to each other in the business setting, the more helpful you will become. Usually the key to understanding the business relationships is examining family relationships.

*"What additional information would be important for me to understand in order to assist your family or business?"*

This is known as a "catch all" question. Sometimes in a structured interview setting, the interviewee has a point he or she would like to share with the interviewer, but the opportunity never occurs. This question is an open invitation to the interviewee to interject anything that may be on his or her mind, but hasn't yet been verbalized. Never leave an interview without posing a catch-all question. Who knows, the most important bit of information of the whole interview might be hanging in the balance.

In addition to these questions, two more important bits of information must be obtained. Ask each individual what his or her objectives are related to four important areas of their life—personal, family, business and financial—and whether or not these objectives have already been achieved.

Some of the objectives included in the fact-finder apply directly to the business owner or owners, but it's important to secure the basic information from all interviewees. The purpose is to be able to eventually organize all the family data obtained into meaningful categories grouped by overall objectives. This task will be described more fully in the next chapter.

The key objectives to ask about can be found in the fact-finder included in the appendix, but here are just a few examples. Ask, *"Is it an important objective of yours…"*

Personal:

*"To obtain financial security during your life?"*

*"To maintain flexibility during your life?"*

Family:

*"To minimize potential family conflicts?"*

*"To achieve the above and maintain flexibility?"*

The objective statements continue into the areas of Business and Financial. The associated page of the fact-finder, Objectives Achieved, provides equally important information.

The goal of this series of objective statements is to establish the extent to which the owners and family members agree that the objectives in question have already been identified and met. Again, the information obtained from each individual is important, but the real payoff comes in contrasting the responses of the owner with those of other family members.

Although the fact-finder questions are geared toward the business owner, they can be adapted to suit the individual interviewee. For example, if the interviewee is one of the children in the family, "Is it an important objective of yours to pass the business intact to your heirs?" becomes "Is it an important objective of yours to see that the business passes to you (or you and your siblings) intact?"

Refocusing the questions to suit the interview in this way not only gets you the important information you need from the owner, it also gives you insight into what the other family members think of each objective. This will allow you to contrast the desires of the owner to those of the heirs. Differences in perception of these objectives by the parties involved will provide valuable information as to how the new wealth transfer plan needs to be designed.

## Setting the Stage for the Interviews

Advisors interested in becoming Wealth Transfer Specialists sometimes ask me about the attitudes of the family members to being interviewed. How do the family members react to the idea?

Well, many family members have told me they could hardly believe their parents had hired an outside person to hear what they had to say about the family and the business. It was a pleasant surprise to many of the children to learn their parents were interested in their concerns and opinions. They were especially surprised their parents were willing to pay someone to learn about their needs and wants. The results are very productive. In addition, I've found that the bonding that occurs as a result of the practice is of value to everyone and frequently sets the stage for family and business meetings for the rest of their lives. Contrast that with the traditional planning done in secrecy without any constructive input from family members.

Considering the importance of the individual family member interviews, how can you be certain you will get the information you need? Well, here are some of my thoughts.

### Identify the ground rules.

Before the interviews begin, make certain the current owner completely agrees with the interview concept and supports it without reservation. It will be very helpful if the current owner expresses his or her support personally to the individual family members. Family members must have assurance they are free to be open and honest in their responses.

Close in importance is the guarantee of confidentiality. This is primarily your job. Assure (and reassure) each family member that the issues discussed in the individual interviews will remain confidential—and then keep that promise. Breaking confidence will be the end of your role as an objective, trusted family Wealth Transfer Specialist. The owner must also understand your position as a confidant and not expect or pressure you to reveal the information you learn during the interview process.

Everyone involved should also understand, however, that the information gained in the interviews will be shared in a general way in designing the new wealth transfer plan. All issues uncovered during the interviews will be incorporated into the recommendations for the new wealth transfer plan in a way that respects each individual's privacy.

Fear of punishment or retribution for expressing one's views must be eliminated in order for the interviews to be meaningful. Interviews where the interviewee is guarded and reluctant to share true feelings will yield little or no useful information.

*Location.*

Where the individual interviews are held also will have an impact. Ideally, they should be conducted in a setting where the interview can be accomplished without interruption. Your office or the interviewee's home or office is fine if it offers sufficient privacy.

*Atmosphere.*

The environment is a critical factor. The place where the interview is to be conducted should be private, quiet and conducive to a thoughtful dialog. The interviewee must be relaxed and unpressured in order to feel comfortable baring his or her soul about the family and business. Make it as easy as possible for the interviewee to participate.

Family members to be included. All adult family members and their spouses will be included in the individual interviews. If you sense it will be difficult to uncover a spouse's concerns because of the domineering nature of the other spouse, it may be necessary to interview them separately. In order to reduce the possibility of in-laws becoming outlaws; it is imperative in-laws be included in the interviews.

At the end of the family interviews, you should have a good feel for the needs, goals, hopes and dreams the individual family members have regarding the business. You also will begin to see how the family interacts and get a feel for some of the family dynamics that impact the business.

## Step 2: Determine Family Objectives

Step two of the Model is to document the family's goals related to the business and personal wealth transfer. This is a fairly simple concept, but it can frequently be difficult to pull together.

The trick to identifying the family's objectives is that they are not likely written down anywhere, and family members may not even be able to verbalize them. Rather, they are contained within the mountain of information you have developed by interviewing the family members and examining the current wealth transfer plan.

You identify the family goals by working through the interview information, studying the personal and business legal and financial documents, and considering the input from the other family advisors. Your goal in this step is to discover what the entire family's goals really are—not what the owner or a family member thinks they are.

Discovering the real family goals can be complicated because many times they are part of someone's hidden agenda. For example, although a business owner might say there is no gender bias in the business, the truth might be that the existing plan clearly demonstrates such a bias by providing the business go to an unqualified son in the family rather than a well-qualified daughter. This is an example of a real family goal in conflict with a stated goal. Your job is to identify the real goal.

A case in point is an Arizona business owner, Rudy, who had a daughter who was active in the business. Sally was married to Bill who, over time, learned the business and eventually rose to CEO. Rudy planned to have Bill take over the business some day. When it was discovered that Bill was having an affair with another woman, the couple divorced, and Rudy asked him to leave the business. Sally became more involved in the management of the business, and because of her willingness to assume greater responsibility, eventually became CEO herself.

As long as Bill was in the picture, Rudy did not see Sally as an important part of the management team because of his gender bias. When circumstances changed and Sally had a chance to show what she was capable of, it became apparent that she was qualified to be heir apparent. In this case, the goal was to keep the business in the family, and gender bias blinded the owner to the obvious choice—his own daughter. It's interesting that it took a family disaster to illuminate her abilities.

In a case like this, you must examine the situation carefully. After all, your job is to help the business develop a plan for business wealth transfer that is in the best interest of both the family and the business. Placing the future of the business in the hands of an unqualified individual could doom whatever well-intentioned plan is developed. This true story illustrates the importance of the Specialist uncovering the real objectives of family members and aligning them with realistic and sensible plans for the future.

## Discovering Objectives

To begin, first organize the family data you've accumulated into broad categories. These should be centered on the objectives you uncovered during the individual family member interviews. Organizing the data in this way will help you see where the current and future owners agree and where they disagree. Let's review the objective statements from the fact-finder and analyze some possible responses.

*To maintain financial security during your lives.*

If the owner is a first-generation entrepreneur, he or she might be an inherent risk-taker. That's a common personality trait for a mover and shaker. The second-generation future owner, on the other hand, might be inclined to "manage" the business with less risk-taking with the goal of providing long-term financial security for his family.

The opposite also could be true. The current business owner, contemplating retirement, might be inclined to back off on risk-taking so as to provide a secure retirement while Junior, fresh out of college with all kinds of new ideas, wants to make a bold leap into the future. The important point to understand is that there are no right or wrong answers to these issues, merely opinions about the attitudes of the various players that must be documented and understood before planning begins in earnest.

*To maintain flexibility during your lives.*

Most people will probably agree that a certain amount of flexibility in their planning for the future is a good idea. But how important is that to each individual? Critical or just a good idea?

*To minimize potential family conflicts.*

Again, most people would probably agree with this objective—but to what extent? Does peace in the family mean sacrificing business objectives if necessary? Does it mean some family members practice passive-aggressive behavior patterns, saying nothing about problems until they finally get fed up and then blow up? What does it mean to each family member to minimize potential family conflicts? An important part of your job is to find out!

*To treat your heirs fairly upon your demise.*

*To treat your heirs equally upon your demise.*

These two objectives appear near identical at first glance. Nevertheless, they are different, and the difference should be explored with each family member. What "feels" fair to each person? Is it fair if Jane gets the business and John receives cash instead? Does it make sense to leave two children one-half ownership in the family business in order to treat them equally when one of them is not active in the business and doesn't want to be? These are critical questions for both the owners and the heirs. Each may have an entirely different view of equal versus fair. Probe for the feelings behind the responses.

*To gradually turn over the operation of the business to your business heirs.*

This one can be loaded. Dad might want to turn the business over to son, but feels he can't because the son simply isn't ready to take over. While there can be legitimate concerns about readiness of the next generation, these concerns sometimes border on the irrational.

The Brown family is a case in point. The family had a three-generation history of alcohol abuse. The current Brown parents, however, successfully gave up alcohol after many years of abuse and determined that no family or non-family employees would be permitted to use alcohol at home or at the site of the family's business.

One day Joe, the father, found evidence that his son, John, and his new wife, Sherrie, had consumed alcohol. This upset Joe to the extent that he required his son to submit to periodic, unannounced urine tests at a local clinic as a condition of remaining with the family firm. Obviously, this totally destroyed any trust remaining between the two. This was probably a case of a misplaced concern or overreaction, but right or wrong, in Joe's mind John was not fit to run the business because of his insistence on defying company policy. There was no way Joe could begin to gradually turn the operation over to him.

Again, asking about this objective is critical. Even if there are no issues like the one facing Joe and John, transferring the operation of the business to the next generation is a very big decision. Under the best of circumstances, there are many issues to consider, such as developing the skills of the potential new owner so the transition will be successful.

Interviewing both the owner and future owner might also reveal another common malady. Dad talks about retiring and passing the business to son, but somehow it never gets beyond the talking stage. In that case, it may be dad who has to confront his own feelings about giving up control—something many entrepreneurs find very difficult to do.

*To pass the business intact to your heirs.*

This may feel like you are asking the obvious, but it's important to establish that this is a real objective. Later, when the recommendations are prepared, you must show that the current plan for wealth transfer will not accomplish this goal, whereas the plan you have designed does. If the current owner would be satisfied with just passing the land intact and you don't realize that fact, your recommendations will miss the mark.

*Create a more business-like approach.*

We discussed in the last chapter the importance of understanding how the family uses the business. This objective gets at that point. In many cases, the family may not even realize they treat the business in a non-business way. If the children grow up thinking that anytime they need something they can just use the business credit card, what does that say about the business systems in place?

Asking the question and probing about business practices may open the family member's eyes. And, after all, if the day-to-day operation of the business is "shoot from the hip," how do you think the transfer plan will play out? For the wealth transfer plan to work, it must be taken seriously. If business operations have not been taken seriously up to this point, this is a good time to get the subject on the table. Developing a new transfer plan is a critical stage in the life of the family and business.

*To minimize your estate taxes.*

Like practically everyone else, business owners do not enjoy paying unnecessary taxes. Again, the answer to this question may seem obvious, but the response may actually have more to do with the perception of loss of control issue than owing taxes. Your recommendations need to address this point, and you'll want to reflect the feelings and opinions of family members.

*To minimize administration costs at death.*

Ditto the above. Why wouldn't the family want to do this? They probably would—but let's have it stated for the record.

*To facilitate gifts to your heirs.*

Gifts are one subject that many people know very little about. The reaction to the idea is often very negative. "You're suggesting I give away my property or possibly my control of the business. I don't think I like that idea!"

It may take a bit of educating your clients, but gifting, of course, can be a very effective way to transfer family wealth. Issues like control of the business can be factored in very easily. The important thing is that the issue is raised and the possibility placed on the table.

*To achieve the above objectives while retaining flexibility.*

Again, why would the family not want this? The concept is important to raise, however, because your primary objectives are to create a plan that works for the family now and to then follow up periodically to make certain it continues to meet the needs of the family and the business. Discussing this objective prepares the family to accept the long-term relationship you intend to maintain.

Step two of the Model is complete when you are convinced that you understand what the family members' expectations are for the business and have assured yourself that those expectations have passed a reality check.

Obviously, in order to conduct effective interviews, you must be totally familiar with the contents of the fact-finder and the nature of the information you are obtaining. Study the fact-finder and make it your own. Add notes in the margins, highlight areas you want to concentrate on in particular, and come prepared with a legal pad or other resource so you can expand your note taking beyond the confines of the fact-finder, if necessary. Remember there is no award for the neatest fact-finder. There is only a reward for the best information obtained. It comes later—when the new wealth transfer plan is accepted because it is so complete and suits the family and business needs so perfectly!

## Step 3: Analyze Current Plan

A good place to begin step three is to gather all the owner's personal and business financial documents. The initial goal is to understand how the business is currently structured and why. A brief history of the business also will be useful. Most businesses start with a single entrepreneur and then evolve into a family partnership or other multiple-owner structure. It will be extremely helpful to know what the driving forces are behind any restructuring of the business. In addition, it's critical to understand the current structure: who owns the company? Who manages it day-to-day? Who are the key people—family and non-family?

An obvious source of information about the existing transfer plan (or lack of it) is the owner himself. As part of your interviews of the owner, it's imperative that you find out how the current plan is structured and why. Is the current plan still a viable option, or was it based on information or assumptions that have changed over time? Was the plan developed after consultation with other family members, or was it constructed in secrecy? Were tax issues a driver in the development of the plan, or was it more centered around control of the business? Who helped design the current plan?

Of course, to fully understand how the existing wealth transfer plan works, it is necessary to understand any legal, tax and financial documents involved. This may mean a meeting with the client's attorney, financial advisor and/or accountant to review documents and the strategy used to develop the current plan.

It also will be helpful to describe for the other advisors the process you intend to use for developing a new plan. Their help will be crucial as the new plan is developed and implemented, and it is vital that you establish a trusting relationship with them early. You must be perceived as part of the same team. Keep in mind that while you think of the owner and family as your client, the other advisors see only the owner as the client. All the while you are developing a new plan, the other advisors are asking themselves "Is this in the best interest of my client, the owner?"

Keeping the other advisors fully informed as the Process unfolds and always treating them with professional courtesy helps assure their support throughout. To try to eliminate any of them or skirt around them in order to avoid their input is a grave mistake. Every team needs a quarterback, and as chief coordinator and motivator, you would be the logical choice to play that role. However, that does not mean you get to run the ball yourself on every play. A team player makes certain everyone understands the play and everyone does his or her part.

### The family/business culture

Part and parcel to understanding the current wealth transfer plan is to develop an understanding of how the family uses the business. For example, is working in the business seen as a birthright or must individual family members earn their position in the company? Do family members treat the business as a "cash cow," or are there strict business practices that separate the business goals from the individual family members needs? Is the business simply seen as "dad's" thing with other family members having little or no involvement in it, or is it truly a family operated enterprise?

Another term for all of this might be discovering the business "culture." As you investigate the culture, keep in mind that a typical closely-held business is sometimes a very complicated mix of family and business culture. Generally speaking, you won't be able to understand one without some context of the other.

As you prepare to conduct the individual family member interviews, keep in mind this will not be "strictly business." Be prepared to deal with family issues such as personality conflict, substance abuse, sibling rivalries and other difficult aspects of family life. When these issues surface, by all means don't avoid them. Understanding the family dynamic will provide deep insight into why the business operates the way it does and why the existing business transfer plan is structured as it is. *To know the family is to better understand the business.*

One of the most telling aspects of the business culture is the ownership and compensation structure. Many family businesses address the issue of "equality" among family members, especially siblings, by having equal ownership and/or paying everyone the same salary—regardless of their contribution to the business success. When this is the case, it indicates a probable lack of a "firewall" between family and business needs. Successful businesses usually pay employees based on their value to the firm. Taking the easy way out—having all the children own equal shares of the business or paying all the children equally regardless of their contribution to the success of the business—indicates an unwillingness to address family issues separately from business strategies. If the business pays family members without regard to their value, there no doubt will be other unsound business practices in place as well. It is critical to identify these and consider them in planning for the future of the business.

### Financial strength of the business

The financial strength of the business is another important consideration. Here again, how the family treats the business wealth will say volumes about the interaction of family and business. The business owner's personal and business financial statements from the last couple of years should be sufficient to give you insight into this aspect. Permission to discuss business and personal finances with other advisors is a must. Many times these professionals have additional information to share over and above what appears in the printed financial reports.

Obviously, sharing information about compensation and financial strength can be difficult for some owners. This single action, probably more than anything else they do, signals the degree of trust the owners have in you as an advisor. It goes without saying that establishing trust is the very first step in building an effective relationship. As we discussed in the previous chapter, the key to developing trust is open, honest communication about your intentions as a Specialist. Establishing a trusting relationship is rule number one. If obtaining financial information is a problem, refer to rule number one!

### Nonfamily key employees

Another very important aspect of understanding the current state of the business is to examine the business with regard to any nonfamily managers and/or key people. Here again, compensation can be a good barometer of family and business interaction. Are there any nonfamily managers or key people who are paid more than some family members? Again, over paying family members versus key people can be an indication of the lack of a business/family firewall.

Nonfamily key persons offer other opportunities. Many times these are talented individuals who help the business succeed, but they are also often loyal to one or more of the business owners and, in many cases, close confidants. The non-family key person often knows a lot about the business, the family's relationship to it and has a unique third-party perspective of it all. They are also often able to deal with difficult family members, or they wouldn't be where they are. An individual who has survived and even prospered in your client's family business can provide a wealth of valuable information. Here again, the owners must approve of your contact with the non-family key persons, and the key people must be comfortable with you and your objectives.

Throughout this discussion we have been assuming the business has an existing plan for transfer of ownership. Of course, many businesses have never formally addressed this issue. It's like writing a will or going to the dentist. Practically everyone agrees it's a good idea, but it can be painful, and it's very easy to put off.

Nevertheless, all businesses do have an ownership wealth transfer plan—they just may not know it. As with a personal will, if you don't create one, no problem—the state, as you know, has one for you. It just may not be what you had in mind.

### Classic cases of failure to plan

I am reminded of a client of mine who grew a successful business with his brother. He was unwilling even in later life to include his wife in the business. He always told her he didn't need her help, and besides, her job was to raise their three daughters, his job was to manage the business. I reminded him, to no avail, that some day he might not be here and asked how his widow would manage the business affairs given she has had no experience with the business. Shortly after our discussion, he died in his sleep, leaving his widow in a partnership with his brother who was a confirmed alcoholic. The widow came to my office one day and let me know in strong language that she was very angry about being so ill prepared to handle the business affairs while dealing with an alcoholic brother-in-law partner. This, in my opinion, is a perfect example of the "no plan" plan. Do nothing and hope everything somehow works out. It rarely—if ever—does.

Being famous and wealthy doesn't guarantee a plan is in place either. The Dec. 16, 1979, edition of The Arizona Daily Star ran a story about the intestate transfer of the property of a well-known rancher, the Duke. John Wayne, it seems, was also one of those procrastinators we just discussed. The article described some of the problems Duke's family was going through trying to settle his estate. The actor's son, Michael Wayne, was quoted in the article as saying, "My father had never done anything with estate planning, although he was urged to, so the taxes have created a burden for the estate." Wouldn't you have thought that the Red River Land Co., Wayne's ranch and the largest privately owned cattle-feeding operation in the nation at the time, would have had a wealth transfer plan? The ranch ended up being sold in order to create the necessary liquidity to pay off estate costs.

Because of your background of technical knowledge, you will be able to describe for the business owner just what sort of plan your state has in mind for the business if he or she steps out of it unexpectedly without having a wealth transfer strategy. The state's intestacy laws may create a very different ownership transfer outcome than the family expected. Knowledge of this fact might just motivate the owners to take that trip to the lawyer's office that they have been procrastinating about (with your new plan under their arm, of course).

## Completing Phase I

Phase I of the Model is complete when you have a thorough understanding of the family's goals and dreams for the business and also fully understand the current wealth transfer plan. Because this early detective work is so important to the success of the practice, make certain it is completed accurately and completely. The work done in Phase I sets the stage for the rest of the Model.

In the next chapter we will begin Phase II of the Model by examining some of the various options available for transferring wealth.

## Chapter 4 summary points:

In this chapter we discussed the first three steps in the FBR Model:

❖  **Step 1: Interview all family members**

  ·Who should be interviewed

  How to conduct the interviews

❖  **Step 2: Determine the family's objectives**

  Use data from interviews to organize family goals

  Determine which goals have already been achieved

  Determine which goals are yet to be achieved

❖  **Step 3: Analyze current plan**

  Use data from interviews and input from other trusted family advisors to identify the current plan for the future of the business

  Determine the "culture" of the family and business

  Determine financial strength of the business

  Consult with non-family key employees

# Chapter 5

## Phase II: Develop a New Wealth Transfer Plan

*First comes thought; then organization of that thought, into ideas and plans; then transformation of those plans into reality. The beginning, as you will observe, is in your imagination.*

*—Napolean Hill*

At this point in the Model, you should have a good understanding of the current plan for transfer of the family's wealth and business interest and insights into some of the family dynamics that could affect the success of the new plan. It's now a matter of taking that knowledge, adding the technical expertise you already have about wealth transfer planning and throwing in more than just a dash of creativity—that's the goal of Phase II. The plan you design must be custom fit for your family clients. No boilerplate approaches. This is where you determine the objectives that have not already been achieved. If you have followed my earlier advice and are charging a value-added fee for your work, this, in large part, is where it is earned.

### Step 4: Determine Alternative Transfer Options

There are many ways family wealth, including business wealth, can be transferred to succeeding generations. We will briefly review some of the most commonly used here.

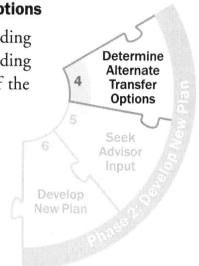

*Wills and Trusts*

Obviously, the current business owner can simply provide for the disposition of the business interest through terms of a will or revocable living trust. In some cases, this is the preferred method of dealing with wealth transfer because it has the comforting effect of feeling as though something has been accomplished, when in fact, nothing really happens until the current owner dies—at which time he isn't going to be around to face the consequences.

The problem, of course, with simply bequeathing ownership of a business by will or trust is that most sizable estates face a liquidity problem at some point. Simply naming a new owner for the business without providing liquidity to make sure the plan works is futile. It becomes a good news/bad news scenario. The good news is dad left you the business—the bad news is it has to be sold to pay taxes and other expenses.

On the plus side, the will/trust plan does permit the current owner to continue to maintain full control of the business during his lifetime—no doubt another reason for its wide appeal.

*Buy-sell Agreement*

This is a very effective tool for business wealth transfer. In essence, it is a legally binding agreement between the current owner and the potential new owner to transfer the business ownership at death, or under other specific conditions, to the new owner at an agreed-upon price or formula. When used in conjunction with other estate planning techniques, this approach can save the business, provide estate liquidity and allow for fair treatment of all business and non-business heirs.

The one drawback to the buy-sell arrangement is the need for cash to fund the buy-out. There are a number of ways to accomplish this—loans, sinking fund, installment payments, etc., but the solution of choice is sufficient life insurance purchased by the potential new owner on the life of the owner. The very problem that causes the need for cash, the death of the owner, also creates the funds necessary to meet the need. Once the estate of the deceased business owner consists largely of cash, dividing it up among business and non-business heirs is relatively easy.

The problem with this solution is the cost of life insurance. Often you are talking about a young person with limited assets needing to purchase large amounts of life insurance on an older person. There are ways to address that issue, but, nevertheless, it looms as a challenge for the insurance/financial advisor.

### Lifetime Sale

Another way to transfer the family business to a new generation of owners is to sell to them using installments while the current owner is still alive.

This can be a very attractive option if the owner is willing to sell. Often, however, it's very difficult for most entrepreneurs to turn over the reins of the business and fade into the sunset.

I heard of a case from another family business advisor that makes the point perfectly. A second-generation owner was complaining that his father, the former business owner, was living a "seagull retirement." When asked to explain he said, "Well, every winter he flies south for a few months, and every spring he flies back up here, hovers over the business and poops on everything!"

The urge for many entrepreneurs to constantly look over the new owner's shoulder and interfere is extremely hard to resist—making the success of this plan difficult.

In addition, a lifetime buy-out means that cash has to come from somewhere. If the buy-out is to come from current business profits, it could produce quite a strain on the business and, in the end, may even threaten its existence.

### Private Annuity

Here is another attractive alternative. The business is transferred to the new owner or owners in exchange for a guaranteed lifetime income to the current owner. It essentially converts the business into a retirement plan for the current owner—hence its appeal.

Like the lifetime sale, however, the money usually has to come from business. Using profits from the business has the drawbacks discussed earlier. In addition, the plan could backfire on the new owner if the lifetime payments finance a "seagull retirement."

### Reorganize the Business

This technique usually consists of creating more than one class of stock in the business so that non-controlling stock can be given to heirs while the voting stock is maintained by the current owner. This arrangement permits some of the business wealth to transfer, but does not result in loss of control by the owner.

A related technique is to create a family limited partnership where limited partnership interests are given or sold to the next generation while the controlling general partnership interest is retained by the current owner.

These techniques can help limit the size of the transfer problem by moving the future increase in business value to the next generation. At least the problem does not continue to get bigger every year. The drawback is that the business interest held by the owner still has to be resolved at some point—which means that the need for cash in the future does not go away entirely.

### Gifts

Another obvious solution for transferring business ownership is for the current owner or owners to transfer portions to the next generation using gifts. If gifts are within the annual exclusion and lifetime exemption limits, this plan can avoid or reduce transfer taxes. However, the amount of the annual gift tax exclusion is relatively low, which means it may take years before a significant percentage of the business can be given away. If the business continues to grow in the meantime, the plan may end up being "one step forward, two steps back."

The other consideration is that while estate taxes may be eliminated in the future, existing gift tax laws have largely remained intact. Gifting may become a much less desirable way to transfer wealth in the future compared to bequests at death. However, tax laws are an ever-moving target so transfer strategies require regular review.

### Philanthropy

Families interested in gifts to charities can benefit from including philanthropy in a wealth transfer plan. Using a technique called a "charitable buy-sell," for example, the owner gives all or part of the business interest to a charity or charitable trust, receiving an immediate income tax deduction for doing so. Since the charity does not want to operate a business, it will attempt to immediately sell. Logical buyers, of course, may be family members. This can be a very effective way to benefit the owner, the charity and family members all in one fell swoop. The chapter on philanthropy treats this subject in more detail and also discusses other ways charitable giving can benefit families by establishing a win-win plan.

### Planning Alternatives

The alternatives discussed above are typical of those available for wealth transfer planning. All have their good and bad points. The Specialist must sort through the options available and identify those that do the best job of addressing the needs of the family members and assist them in achieving their collective goals.

## Step 5: Seek Input from Owner Advisors

Recall that a critical objective for the individual family member interviews was to gather information about each family member's needs, desires and expectations related to the future of the business and their

role in it. Before beginning the development of a new
plan, be absolutely certain you are clear about
all of the family members' concerns. If you are
not sure about something one or more of the
family members said (or didn't say), take
the time to visit again with them and clear
up any misunderstandings or fill in any
blanks. Designing a transfer plan ideally
suited to the circumstances of the particular family you are working with is the signature of a professional Wealth Transfer
Specialist.

Once you are clear on the family's per-
spective, it is time to touch base once again with the owner's trusted advisors. This time your primary objectives will be to get information about
current plans and their input into the design of a new wealth transfer
plan. In large part, of course, their input will reflect their professional
area of expertise. Keep in mind, however, that as trusted advisors, these
individuals may or may not have been privileged to many "family secrets"
over the years. In addition, they also may have been involved in previous planning efforts and understand the business history. Seeking their
counsel concerning potential problems or conflicts can be very useful in
the planning process.

For example, suppose your individual family member interviews lead
you to believe that a particular family member may have a problem such
as substance abuse that is causing a strain on the family and complicat-
ing transfer planning. You might want to check out your suspicions with
other family advisors. Chances are, if such a problem really does exist,
one or more of them have dealt with it in some form or another in the
past. The experience and insights of other trusted advisors into family
relationships and communication problems can be very helpful.

It is important, however, that your discussions with other advisors not
be viewed as gossip or "carrying stories." Only share your concerns with

other family advisors who are pledged to keeping confidences and make certain they understand you are also concerned with the privacy of all the individual family members. Remember that advisors are often not familiar with other family members because they view only the owner as their client. If you are perceived as someone sincerely willing to help your mutual clients, interested in these personal matters only to the extant they impact on the transfer planning, you will receive the cooperation of the other family advisors.

Many advisors I've worked with have told me they appreciate my bringing the entire family together in the planning process. It helps greatly to have everyone understand the planning complexities. Other advisors have thanked me for assisting in implementing the new plan in a timely manner.

Many family advisors have told me that, as a result of the parents' willingness to include the children in the planning procedure, the children themselves eventually became their clients. The relationship established between the advisor and the entire family, by working through the process together, pays many dividends.

Your clients will also appreciate your working effectively with other trusted advisors. Here's an excerpt from a letter I received from a client that makes the point.

*Dear Karl,*

*"During the past several months since my rather severe health problems became evident, I have had time to consider and appreciate the wealth transfer planning service you rendered me in giving me the added "push" that was needed to get something done on our estate planning problem.*

*As you probably remember when I first discussed the problem with you in Denver, I made it clear that I had a very intelligent, qualified attorney of my own that would have to work with you on any advice or action that we would accept. It was very gratifying to me that you, my attorney and accountant worked so well together and came up with a wealth transfer plan that looks like it will accomplish our objectives.*

*We have enjoyed working with you, Karl, and your staff on this project. Your knowledge, experience and ability are sincerely appreciated. Should any business want to contact me about your services, feel free to have them call me."*

*Sincerely,*

*Bill*

### Ethics and the FBR Model

While we're on the subject of working with other advisors and respecting confidences, let's expand the discussion slightly to address the broader subject of ethics as it related to the Model.

If you are a member of the Society of Financial Services Professionals (formerly the American Society of CLU and ChFC), you subscribe to its code of ethics. The professional pledge of the Society best summarizes the code:

*"In all my professional relationships, I pledge myself to the following rule of ethical conduct: I shall, in light of all conditions surrounding those I serve, which I will make every conscientious effort to ascertain and understand, render that service which, in the same circumstances, I would apply to myself."*

The relationship of the pledge to the "golden rule" is easy to see.

Other professions have similar ethical requirements. The Preamble to the Rules of Professional Conduct from the state of Idaho is representative of the code of ethics for the legal profession.

*"In all professional functions a lawyer should be competent, prompt and diligent. A lawyer should maintain communication with a client concerning the representation. A lawyer should keep in confidence information relating to representation of a client..."*

In other words, lawyers should be knowledgeable and stay in touch with their client and keep confidential information confidential. The Rules of Professional Conduct themselves cover hundreds of pages, but to paraphrase: lawyers are charged with being competent advisors who put the best interests of their client ahead of their own, while honoring confidences and keeping their client informed.

The American Institute of Certified Public Accountants Code of Professional Conduct is extensive, but contains wording similar to the ethics codes of the attorney and financial services professional.

Interpretive comments within the code define the requirements for due care.

*"The quest for excellence is the essence of due care. Due care requires a member to discharge professional responsibilities with competence and diligence. It imposes the obligation to perform professional services to the best of the member's ability with concern for the best interest of those for whom the services are performed and consistent with the profession's responsibility to the public."*

Bankers and trust officers likewise are bound by a code of ethics that stresses the need for confidentiality. Here's a portion:

*"Financial institutions should limit employee access to personally identifiable information to those with a business reason for knowing such information. Financial institutions should educate their employees so that they will understand the importance of confidentiality and customer privacy. Financial institutions should also take appropriate disciplinary measures to enforce employee privacy responsibilities."*

The bottom line is that all professional advisors are under an obligation to treat the client with respect by honoring confidentiality and pursuing solutions that clearly are in the client's best interests. Nothing less than full and impartial application of the "golden rule" will do. Keep your ethical obligations in mind throughout the procedure. You will be better off in every way—including the diminished likelihood that you will be placing a call to your errors and omission or malpractice insurer.

## Step 6: Develop New Plan

Now that you have a suitable collection of information and feelings related to both family and business, it's time to pull it all together and forge a workable wealth transfer plan.

This is the analytical phase of the Model. It's the point where the Specialist calls upon his or her technical expertise as well as the technical expertise of the other family advisors and uses it to formulate a solution. Without the Model as a guide, most professional advisors jump to this step early in the first interview. Hopefully, you can see the value of the preceding steps and have a feel for how they develop the critical information needed in completing this step successfully.

Reduced to its basic components, this step is essentially taking what you know about the family's objectives, eliminating the objectives already achieved through prior planning, and formulating a plan that addresses those objectives still unmet. Sounds simple, doesn't it?

Of course, it is often anything but simple. Not only are there financial, legal and tax issues to be addressed, there are also a myriad of personal issues—many that are very important to family members—that must be addressed. For example, if a logical solution for business succession happens to be passing the business to the oldest son at the death of the owner, a simple buy-sell agreement would seem to fill the bill. But what if a son-in-law, also active in the business, feels he should have some owner-ship? What if the daughter in the family is interested in owning the business and is clearly qualified to manage it? What if the daughter is a better choice than the son is? What if the son has potential to succeed as the eventual business owner, but currently has a lack of knowledge or skills or both? What if a key employee is a better choice for eventual successor?

These questions and others indicate potentially serious challenges to the Specialist in the new plan development. However, absent the spade-work accomplished in the early steps of the Model, many of these issues would not even be on the planner's radar screen. This is why the fist five steps of the Model are so critical. Without knowledge of the issues hinted at by the questions above, the typical advisor has practically no chance of designing a solution that actually will work!

It's not the purpose of this book to examine all possible business wealth transfer planning techniques in detail—although many will be addressed in some detail in a later chapter. Suffice it to say that the technical train-ing the Specialist possesses—the "competence" part—comes into play during this step. The crucial distinction between the Specialist's approach and that of the typical family business advisor is that the Specialist pur-sues various options fully informed of the real family objectives, not just the desires articulated by the business owner.

### Capturing Plan Details

Once the technical solution or solutions have been identified by the Specialist, they must be put into a format that will be suitable for discus-sion in a family retreat setting—the topic of our next chapter.

That means the ideas must be well thought out and expressed in lay person's language. In addition, the ideas must be presentable in a format that lends itself to a facilitated group discussion. The best way to do that is to use the FBR software specifically designed for this purpose.

## FBR Software

Following is an example of how easily the software organizes the objec-tives portion based on the input from the family interviews. The output of the software is a combination of information manually entered and already existing material that applies to many estate and business plan-ning strategies.

# Planning Objectives
# of Gary and Phyllis Smith

(SAMPLE)

**Personal:**

- To maintain financial security during your lifetime.
- To maintain flexibility during your lifetime.

**Family:**

- To minimize potential family conflict.
- To treat heirs fairly upon your demise.
- To achieve the above while maintaining flexibility.

**Business:**

- To gradually turn over the operation of the business to your business heirs.
- To pass the business intact to your heirs.
- To create a more business-like approach.

**Financial:**

- To minimize your estate taxes.
- To minimize administration costs at death.
- To facilitate gifts to your heirs.

**General:**

- To achieve all of the above objectives while retaining sufficient flexibility to adjust to changing personal and economic situations and estate and gift tax laws.

# Objectives Achieved and Not Achieved

### (SAMPLE)

**OBJECTIVES ACHIEVED**

**Personal:**

- You have the means of remaining financially secure during your lifetime.
- Your current estate plan allows you to maintain flexibility.

**OBJECTIVES NOT ACHIEVED**

**Family:**

- Your current estate plan does not minimize the potential for conflict among family members.
- Your estate plan may not treat your heirs fairly upon your demise.

**Business:**

- You have not arranged your business affairs so as to be able to eventually turn over the actual operation of your business to your heirs and yet retain financial control during your lifetime.
- It may be difficult to pass the business intact to the business heirs and still treat any non-business heirs fairly at your demise because of the nature of your assets.
- You have not created a business-like approach between family members and the business in order to have the business survive and create harmony within the family.

**Financial:**

- The existing wills do not take advantage of substantial changes made in estate and gift tax laws. The Unified Credit will be wasted in the estate of the first spouse to die and needlessly increase the estate tax in the survivor's estate. The estate of the deceased spouse should be divided between a bypass trust that will absorb the Unified Credit and a marital deduction trust that will offset the balance of the estate tax until the death of the second spouse.

- Costs of probate administration will not be minimized under the present plan because most of your assets will pass through probate.
- Your present estate and business plan will not minimize estate shrinkage because the full, appreciated value of all your assets will be included in your estate for death tax purposes.
- Lifetime gifts are not facilitated, as you must give liquid assets or interests in your business, which could result in a loss of control.

Note that the software organizes the major issues in terms of objectives desired, objectives achieved and objectives not achieved. This approach is a logical method for identifying problems—basically the unachieved objectives. The remainder of the report contains suggestions for how to resolve the unmet objectives.

The introduction of the report contains financial statements for the family and the business and other facts about the current wealth transfer plan. The software allows the Specialist to summarize the current personal and business documents for the report. A section at the end of the report contains a glossary of terms that might be unfamiliar to the reader. The complete report, including the glossary, may be anywhere from 30 to 50 pages in length.

The report is bound into booklets and copies distributed to everyone at the family retreat. The report, along with slides, flip-chart drawings and other presentation techniques you employ, will guide the retreat discussions.

The next chapter will discuss in detail how to manage the family retreat and how to use the FBR System report when presenting the new plan to family members.

# Chapter 5 summary points:

In this chapter we discussed steps four, five and six in the FBR Model:

◈ **Step 4: Determine Alternative Transfer Options**

  **Wills and trusts**

  **Buy-sell agreements**

  **Lifetime sale of the business**

  **Gifts and other transfer techniques**

◈ **Step 5: Seek Input from Owner Advisors**

  **Establish an effective working relationship with the other business advisors**

  **Ethics and the FBR Model**

◈ **Step 6: Develop New Plan**

  **Develop the new wealth transfer plan**

  **Use the FBR software to create the presentation document for the new plan**

# Chapter 6

## Phase III: Conduct Family Retreat and Implement New Plan

*Advice is like castor oil, easy enough to give but dreadful uneasy to take.*

—*Josh Billings*

*Ye shall know the truth, and the truth shall make you mad.*

—*Aldous Huxley*

Using the family retreat to present the new plan for wealth transfer is another unique characteristic of our Model. It flows from the principle that the client is the entire family, not just the business owner. The plan could be presented to the owner only, but the family retreat is the only way to be certain that everyone who has a stake in the outcome hears the details of the new plan from the same person, in the same way, at the same time.

With the advantages of the family retreat come a few challenges. Remember all that confidential information developed during the family member interviews and visits with the other family advisors? Well, that information (however, not the source) will be part of the solution presentation. Some of that information may be controversial or difficult for some in the room to hear. Open, honest communication sometimes creates confrontation—and some of the controversial information may have been buried or avoided by some family members for a long time. Old wounds may be reopened and salt poured into them. Fresh wounds may be inflicted. But, in the end, open communication results in establishing a quality family life.

## Step 7: Present New Plan

Having said that, the family retreat has the potential for confrontation—even unpleasantness—it is also often a catharsis of sorts that has the power to break down barriers to communication that may have been stifling family members and negatively affecting family relationships for years.

The family retreat is always an interesting experience, and not without its lighter moments.

A number of years ago I met for two and one-half days with a large family of 31 adults—including three generations—to consider a new wealth transfer plan I had created. During one of the sessions I described the economic value of holding a minority interest in a family-owned business as being insignificant. I indicated the value of such an interest might be even less than the cost of a role of toilet tissue. Imagine the look on my face the next morning when I came into the meeting room and found an abundance of toilet paper at the podium!

## Objectives of the Family Retreat

There are a number of objectives that the Specialist must have in mind while conducting a family retreat:

- Create an atmosphere for open and honest communication
- Revisit the needs and expectations family members have of the business
- Present the new plan in a way that demonstrates how it addresses family needs and expectations
- Obtain agreement from the family members to implement the new plan

### Introduction

The key to the introduction is to open the family dialog and get all the family members involved in the interaction.

Since all family members will have met you during the individual interviews, there is no need to formally re-introduce yourself now. It is important, however, to introduce the agenda for the retreat. Explain how the session will be conducted and what you hope to accomplish. People are more comfortable if they have some idea of what to expect and how the event will proceed. A written agenda can be useful for this purpose. Avoid putting times on the agenda, however, as it will raise tensions if at some point it appears the session is "behind."

After the opening remarks, begin by asking these three questions of each family member in turn.

1. What do you expect from the retreat?
2. What do you admire most about the family and the business?
3. What would you like to see changed?

By responding to each of these non-threatening, open-ended questions, family members have the opportunity to "get their voice into the room" and overcome any initial shyness. This technique assures everyone gets actively involved. It also gives each individual a chance to voice his or her degree of satisfaction with the status quo and hopes for change.

*Review the current plan.*

Continue by reviewing the legal documents and financial statements for the owner and the business. These are summarized in the FBR software report. The goal is to help the family members understand the plan that is currently in place for the transfer of the family's wealth. An understanding of the current plan forms the basis for evaluating the new plan.

*Present the new plan.*

Of course, the initial objective of the retreat is to have all family members leave with an understanding of how the proposed new plan works and how it will preserve and protect the family's personal and business wealth. The skill required of the Specialist in this area is primarily that of an effective facilitator. There are a number of factors to keep in mind.

- *Know your topic.* You must understand all the technical aspects of your proposed plan and all the financial, legal and tax considerations that enter into it.

- *Speak clearly.* Avoid the use of technical jargon. Trying to impress the audience by using legal, tax and financial jargon or slang will only serve to confuse. Try to think back to a time when you knew little or nothing about these technical subjects. How would you have preferred a professional to communicate with you?

  Using technical jargon does not impress your audience with your storehouse of knowledge; rather it creates the impression you are insensitive to their needs. And remember, if they wanted to, the family members could probably dazzle you with technical talk about their business too. There's nothing to be gained by being overly technical. At the same time, don't "talk down" to your audience either. That's another sure turn off.

- *Use facilitation skills.* A facilitator, by definition, facilitates a conversation—meaning the presentation is a dialog, not a monologue or lecture. Include your audience in the discussion by asking frequent "checking questions." Sprinkle your conversation with questions like "Did I make that clear?" "Did I answer your question satisfactorily?" "What do you think of this approach?" "Who can think of another reason why this approach might (or might not) work in this case?"

In other words, work persistently to draw out the members of your audience by asking direct questions at various times during the retreat. Be careful not to embarrass anyone who may be shy about speaking up, but do make a conscious effort to include everyone.

### Encourage involvement.

We've already discussed the fact that everyone in the room may not feel safe or comfortable speaking his or her mind in a group setting. Nevertheless, the Specialist must make the effort to draw out everyone's opinions. If there is an objection to the new plan that is not addressed in the family retreat, it may become part of a hidden agenda that eventually can come back to haunt you. Hidden agendas have a way of festering and have the potential to ultimately scuttle the most carefully designed wealth transfer plan.

When attempting to draw out a shy person, do so tactfully without embarrassing him or her. Ask direct questions about the person's opinions and use frequent checking questions such as, "How does that approach sound to you, Jack?"

### Offer positive feedback.

One of the best ways to encourage participation in a group setting is to respond positively whenever someone offers input. "That's an excellent question, Jill" or, "I'm glad you raised that point, Bill." The quickest way to stifle participation is to offer negative feed back such as "That's not right" or "I wouldn't do it that way."

### Manage conflict.

If the discussion during the retreat becomes heated at some point, it's important to diffuse the tension and get the discussion back on a constructive path. It does no good to allow venting of anger or frustration.

The benefits of "getting it out of one's system" are overrated. Allowing someone to use another person as a verbal punching bag is not helpful and can poison the atmosphere of negotiation and compromise you are trying to develop. Better to resolve the tension by helping all parties involved understand how each will benefit from the new plan.

Judicious use of humor can also be very effective in diffusing tension. Another helpful technique is enlisting the aid of others family members in diffusing tension. Generally, when there is a history of disagreement, someone in the family has traditionally played the role of peacemaker. Identify that person and encourage him or her to participate in the discussion if things begin to feel tense. However, don't permit the peacemaker to simply acquiesce and allow a troublemaker to get his or her way through intimidation or other bullying tactics.

The key is to stress the benefits of the new plan. Everyone will not get exactly what he or she started out wanting, but once members come to understand that their sacrifice is vital to the ongoing success of the business, they usually can accept the new reality. In the end, reason must prevail. If the Model does not result in a plan that secures the long-range future of the business by preserving and protecting the family's wealth, it will have been a failure.

It is critical that the Specialist remain open and unbiased during the entire retreat process. Never become defensive about the details of the new wealth transfer plan. Recognize there may be a need to modify the plan based on the reactions of the family members during the retreat. Of course, the more complete the individual interviews were, the less likely extensive modification will be necessary.

### Obtain agreement to implement.

This is the primary objective of the family retreat. At the end of the retreat the family must be in agreement that the new plan is the right thing to do and will support implementation. The family retreat setting is the best opportunity for obtaining agreement. If the retreat ends without agreement, hidden agendas, coalition building and other power shifting tactics may emerge, potentially destroying chances of ever implementing the new plan.

At the end of the family retreat, everyone should be convinced the new wealth transfer plan, while maybe not perfect, is the best solution for the long-term success of the family and business.

### Summarize family expectations.

Briefly review the responses to the three questions posed at the beginning of the retreat. Determine if the major expectations expressed by the family members have all been met to their satisfaction. Do the recommended changes satisfy the objectives expressed by the individual family members?

### Celebrate victory.

At the close of the retreat, after everyone has accepted the new wealth transfer plan, celebrate the victory. Prepare in advance by planning a party or celebration (appropriate to the family's culture) that will signal the successful end of a long journey. Again, someone in the family may be the "unofficial" party planner for family events. Ask that person to be responsible for the celebration so you can be sure the event will match the family's expectations. You don't want to break out the champagne only to find out most of the family members are non-drinkers!

Make every effort to make the celebration a memorable event. Something very important has happened. The family has successfully negotiated white-water rapids and achieved a major milestone in the history of the family and business. It truly is an accomplishment that calls for a celebration!

As evidence of the potential impact the planning method can have on a family, consider the following excerpt from a letter I received from a client. This is just one example of many similar letters.

*I want to personally thank you from the bottom of my heart for the tremendous job you have done in bringing our family together as one family.*

*Karl, your ability to do this is a great treasure to family-owned businesses. You have done something no one else could have done in bringing all family members together in a common bond to plan for our family wealth transfer.*

*My wife and I and all of our children are very appreciative of your work. I sat there in great amazement listening to our children speak with such clarity and some even made us cry. Your expertise made all this possible.*

*Thank you again,*

*—M. T.*

The experience of openly sharing hopes, dreams and concerns about the family business is cathartic in many cases.

### Add your personal thanks.

The close of the family retreat also signals the end of a major segment of your work as a Specialist. While not completely out of the woods (surprises can still occur), you are through the most difficult steps of the Model. As part of the wrap-up and close of the family retreat, take the time to express your own gratitude for the cooperation you have received from the individual family members. If some have made exceptional contributions to the process, recognize them individually.

If the procedure has resulted in a breakthrough for the family or individual family members, recognize that as well. Of course, in the process, remember to honor confidentiality, and don't embarrass anyone who would prefer not to be the focus of attention.

The business owner may be in line for special praise because he or she is probably the one who has come the farthest distance. Taking deliberate action to plan for turning over the reins of a business can be a very difficult step for the typical entrepreneur, as we've discussed. That sacrifice is an indication of the owner's love and concern for the family and deserves special recognition.

As you can probably imagine, I've experienced a variety of family member behaviors during family retreats. However, the bonding of family members continues to delight me. The willingness of family members to share of themselves and help develop quality relationships, enhance family communications and improve their understanding of the business truly is amazing.

I remember a grandfather who was listening to his grandchildren tell how much they appreciated his hard work, willingness to risk all, and the many sacrifices he made so their lives could be easier. Hearing this was too much for the grandfather who started crying while listening to their expressions of appreciation. By the end of the session, there wasn't a dry eye in the entire room. It's important to have facial tissue available for moments like this.

There are times when old family or business issues surface and anger is demonstrated. At times like that, it's important for the wealth transfer specialist to remain objective while facilitating these concerns. In some cases, where serious issues are affecting the family relationships, I have recommended the family seek out professional help. I once asked a therapist who works with alcohol addiction to attend a family meeting because I had information from my individual meetings that this was a problem affecting the quality of family life and the profitability of the business.

## Step 8: Consider Liquidity Options

At the core of almost every wealth transfer plan is the need for additional liquidity. The discussion about liquidity sometimes takes place during the retreat, but frequently happens after the retreat and generally includes only the individuals directly involved. Liquidity may be needed for estate settlement costs and estate taxes and to facilitate a business buy out. In any case, it's very unusual to find a family business situation where there is sufficient funding already available to fully implement the new plan. Generally, the need for liquidity takes one (or both) of two forms, estate liquidity or business liquidity.

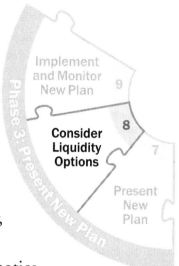

### Estate liquidity.

A very common need in the typical family business situation is a need for liquidity to settle estate costs and taxes. This generally is true because business owners typically reinvest profits back into their business continuously, and as a result, accumulate few liquid assets.

Although subject to change at a moment's notice, estate tax laws generally result in a need for cash at the second death in a married couple's situation. That is because there is an unlimited tax exemption for property passing at death from one spouse to another. At the death of the second spouse, however, when property passes to the next generation, for example, the estate tax becomes payable. This cost, in addition to the other settlement costs such as funeral, debt and last illness expenses, must be paid from estate assets. Since the typical business owner family is "asset rich and cash poor," the need for liquidity arises.

### Business liquidity.

The second major liquidity need for business-owner families usually arises when the ownership of the business interest must change hands. Often this occurs at the death of the business owner. The problem is similar to the estate cash need—the solution requires cash, but the individuals usually have non-liquid assets.

### Providing liquidity.

There are a number of ways to address liquidity needs. Here are a few.

- *Loans.* One source of cash for an estate or business interest purchase is loans. The estate or the business buyer simply approaches a lender and negotiates a loan on acceptable terms. The problem, of course, is the loan plus interest must be paid back. If the estate or individual is short of cash now, carrying indebtedness is not going to be easy. If a loan is used to purchase a business from the deceased owner's estate, the added burden of carrying the debt can seriously cripple the business. In any case, the bank may be reluctant to loan money after the death of the business owner.

- *Installment payments.* In the case of a business buy out, payments can sometimes be made from the cash flow of the business itself. However, like the loan scenario described above, the business cash flow can be seriously affected, jeopardizing the business. In addition, installment payments, like loans, include interest, further increasing the cost.

- *Sinking fund.* In this approach, money is set aside in a relatively risk-free account for later use to pay taxes or purchase the business interest. This plan can work, given enough time. Unfortunately, no one knows when the need for the money will arise. If the current owner dies unexpectedly, for example, there may not be enough in the sinking fund to cover the purchase.

- *Life insurance.* This is often the preferred solution. The death benefit from life insurance provides an immediate infusion of income tax-free cash into the estate or the hands of the business buyer. When the money is used to execute a buy-sell agreement, it usually results in an exchange of the non-liquid business asset in the estate for cash. Potential problems center on the availability of premiums and insurability.

This method solves both problems neatly. The buyer receives the death benefit, turns it over to the estate in exchange for the business interest, and goes on his way as the owner of a business unencumbered by debt. Meanwhile, the estate of the deceased owner has a non-liquid asset converted to cash—usually without tax consequences. The need for liquidity by the business buyer and the estate have both been addressed by a single solution—a buy-sell agreement funded with life insurance on the current business owner.

Providing the liquidity necessary to make the new wealth transfer plan work is an essential component. It cannot be ignored. Sometimes a combination of loans, installment payments and life insurance can be employed as a solution. In any case, the problem must be addressed, or the new plan cannot be implemented.

## Step 9: Implement and Monitor New Plan

The last step in the Model is one that is vitally important to the long-term success of the new wealth transfer plan. No matter how good the plan is, how well thought out it is, how ingenious it is, it won't do anyone any good if it is not fully implemented or is allowed to become ineffective over time.

It seems it should almost go without saying that the plan must be implemented. What sense does it make to spend time, money and energy on a plan and then not implement it? Unfortunately, many well-designed plans are left on the drawing board and never fully implemented. The reasons are many.

One human trait almost all of us share is the tendency to procrastinate. In this regard, business-owner families are no different. The owner information may be gathered, the new plan developed *and the new plan shelved.*

Another reason a plan may never be fully implemented is a variation of "buyer's remorse." After the initial wealth transfer experience fades, the urge to want to "keep things as they are" can return. The business owner may have second thoughts about giving up control after all. A family member may say or do something that irritates the business owner to the point that passing on the business no longer seems like such a great idea. I had one case where a well-meaning friend, who was unaware of the new plan, convinced the owner to rethink his decision. Given enough time, anything can happen!

It is incumbent upon the Specialist to make certain the plan is actually implemented in its entirety. This means going beyond completing the agreement you will be paid to do, such as taking applications for financial products or monitoring new legal documents. You must take responsibility, as architect of the plan, to see that all the pieces of the plan are put into action. That may mean playing the role of mother hen, but it must be done. Sometimes it means going so far as to drive the owner to their advisor's office or driving the advisor to the place of business. Somehow, the plan, in its entirety, must become a reality—or the job is not complete!

Finally, planning for family and business renewal is a journey, not a destination. You never really "arrive." Once the new wealth transfer plan is fully implemented, it must be constantly monitored to make certain it continues to serve the intended purpose. Creating the plan from scratch is by far the most labor-intensive part of the procedure. If you make it all the way through the first eight steps of the Model, you are to be congratulated. However, don't stop there. Follow-through is critical.

If nothing else changes, tax laws will. Will Rogers is said to have quipped "The two certainties of life are death and taxes—but at least death doesn't get worse every time Congress meets!" Maybe death doesn't get worse, but understanding the tax code and keeping up with its periodic changes definitely gets harder all the time. Over the past couple decades there have been dozens of changes to income and transfer taxes. Any one of them could render a wealth transfer plan defective. The Specialist owes the client family constant vigilance in this area. At least yearly, review the plan with the family and verify it is still consistent with the family's goals and that law changes or other factors have not rendered it obsolete. Of course, if the family or business circumstances change, or a major tax revision occurs, the plan must be scrutinized in light of those changes. Such changes may require the help of others on the family's trusted advisor team.

Installing a tracking system for keeping the new wealth transfer plan valid is the last step of the three phases and nine steps in the Model.

But, as noted above, this is not the end of the journey. Frequent contact and regular follow-up with the family and business is required. It just makes good sense for everyone anyway. It maintains your relationship with the family and positions you as a key advisor for the next generation of owners.

In the next chapter we'll summarize where we've been and review the entire Model again for another look at the big picture.

## Chapter 6 summary points:

In this chapter we discussed steps seven, eight and nine in the FBR Model:

◈ Step 7: Present the new plan

   Objectives of the family retreat

   How to conduct a successful family retreat

   Tips and techniques for the family retreat

◈ Step 8: Consider Liquidity Options.

   Estate liquidity versus business liquidity

   Liquidity options

◈ Step 9: Implement and Monitor the New Plan

   Importance of following through with implementation

   Setting expectations for periodic review

# Chapter 7

## Getting Started as a Wealth Transfer Specialist

*Life affords no higher pleasure than that of surmounting difficulties, passing from one step of success to another, forming new wishes and seeing them gratified.*

*—Samuel Johnson*

By now you should have a good feel for our Model, how it works and the obvious advantages it offers the advisor, the business owner and family members. It's time to talk about how one actually goes about getting started as a Wealth Transfer Specialist.

There are basically three areas to be concerned with. The first is to develop the facilitation and mediation skills necessary to work in this environment, the second is to learn and use the FBR System software, and the third is to learn how to market yourself effectively to potential prospects. We'll examine each in turn.

Obviously, every family business advisor must have some "sales" skills. Even the attorney and accountant, who may feel they are not "sales people," must sell themselves and their services to prospects every day. Those that are the best at marketing themselves prosper. Those who are not effective, flounder—often wondering why they don't have more clients. One solution to this dilemma is traditional sales skills training—often based on manipulation techniques. Our process, on the other hand, depends upon effective questioning and active listening skills. Suffice it to say that every family business advisor must be adept at building trusting relationships and persuading individuals to act positively on their recommendations.

For the balance of this discussion, we'll assume that effective communication skills are in place and will concentrate on the facilitation and mediation aspects of getting started as a Wealth Transfer Specialist.

## Facilitation Skills

Earlier, when discussing the family retreat, we discussed briefly the importance of acting as a facilitator rather than a presenter. The difference, in essence, is in the amount of participation on the part of the audience. In a presentation, the presenter talks, and the audience listens (unless and until they fall asleep, that is). A facilitator is someone who draws the audience into active participation using a variety of methods. The family retreat requires facilitation skills.

Here are some of the techniques for becoming an effective facilitator.

### Availability

Make yourself available to the audience before the retreat begins. Don't arrive at the last minute. Be there to help everyone become comfortable before getting started.

### Be prepared

Know your subject backward and forward. Anticipate questions that might arise regarding the new plan, and be prepared to deal with them. You don't want to be embarrassed by having to answer a question with, "Gee, I never thought of that!"

### Consider your appearance

The best rule of thumb is to dress as your audience would expect you to—or a bit better. It's always easy to take off a sport jacket, for example, if you feel you are overdressed. In you are underdressed, however, there is not much you can do except take a hit to your credibility.

If you have never done so, videotape yourself giving a presentation and critique your posture, mannerisms, gestures, facial expressions, eye contact, etc. Ask a spouse or trusted friend to help you with the critique.

### Have a prepared agenda

Everybody appreciates knowing in advance what the agenda is. It helps everyone get in the mood and up to speed about expectations.

### Equipment

Arrive early and make certain all your equipment works as it should. It is always wise to have thought through a "back-up plan" as well—in case something unexpectedly goes wrong with your equipment. For example, make sure you have an extra projector bulb—but be prepared to make your presentation without slides in case your projector ups and dies.

### Attitude

Always project a confident attitude. Don't begin by apologizing for the weather, appearance of the room, your having to use reading glasses, etc. Assume you are the expert in the room on the subject at hand and go for it!

Have an effective opening. Don't wait until you are ready to begin before thinking about your opening. Have a strong opening rehearsed. Opening with humor is good if you can pull it off (don't try it if you are the type that forgets punch lines). In place of humor, a story about how you met the business owner or other personal story about a family member is good. Another effective opener is to begin with a meaningful quotation appropriate for the occasion.

Tell them what you are going to tell them. Tell them. And then tell them what you told them. Lay the groundwork for your presentation so everyone knows what to expect. Anything you can do to relax the audience and demonstrate commonality with them will make for a powerful opening. In any case, your opening should gain everyone's attention, help "break the ice," and be relevant to the subject at hand.

### Express appreciation

Recognize the fact that this family has taken you onto their confidence and placed a high degree of trust in you. Be sure to acknowledge that fact by expressing your appreciation for their cooperation and their willingness to participate in the process.

### Eye Contact

As you work with your audience, be sure you make an effort to make eye contact with everyone in the room at some point. Don't address all your remarks to the owner, for example. Pay attention to all areas of the room and everyone in it. Each person should feel you are addressing him or her personally.

### Focus on the audience

Forget about yourself and focus all your attention on the people in front of you. This is their event—you are merely there to guide them through it. Put the needs of the audience before your own. Schedule regular breaks. A short break every 50 to 60 minutes is usually about right. Much longer than that and you begin to lose some people.

### Use questions

Repeatedly include your audience by asking questions as you discuss the new wealth transfer plan. These are not in the nature of "test" questions. In other words, avoid questions with a yes or no answer or right or wrong answer, rather use open-ended questions that will draw the audience members into a discussion. Questions like "What do you think...," "How do you feel about...," "Who can give me an example of..." These are all questions that require discussion.

Pay compliments. Be careful here, however. All compliments must be sincere. Anything that seems to be insincere flattery is a certain credibility killer. On the other hand, a sincere compliment is always appreciated. However, avoid complimenting anyone on his or her physical appearance. This usually is inappropriate and often comes across as insincere flattery. But if someone gives a good answer or raises a good point, say so!

### Use visuals

Slides or a Power Point presentation add interest to your presentation. Use common sense in designing visuals, however. A couple rules of thumb are:

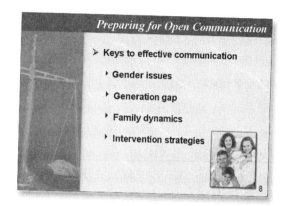

- Use bullets, not paragraphs

- Never use more than two different fonts on a slide

- No more than six words per line and six lines per slide

- No more than two or three colors per slide

- Avoid vertical lettering

- Use contrast to improve readability

- Use upper and lower case letters

- Use appropriate graphics

### Keep the discussion on track

If the discussion strays, an excellent technique for bringing it back is to refer back to a previous point someone made. Say, "I'd like to go back to something Jack said earlier..." and pick up the point and expand on it. You also can use this technique on an individual who is taking the discussion away from the issues at hand. Say, "Something you said a minute ago seems important..." and go back to that point. It will short circuit the current discussion and bring it back to the more important issues at hand.

Unless absolutely necessary, however, don't interrupt a speaker—let the other person talk. Only intervene if the discussion is obviously getting off the track.

## Mediation Skills

In some cases facilitation turns to mediation. As we've discussed, sometimes there are strong feelings or rivalries lurking just below the surface. The retreat discussion may bring some of these to the surface where they must be dealt with. Let's consider a few tips for how to be an effective mediator.

### Know your audience

Do some detective work ahead of time on who might act out during the session or where potential rivalries might exist. You might also develop some of this information during discussions with other advisors about the history of the current plan.

Enlist the aid of a friendly family member who is willing to let you in on some of the straight scoop about the family. However, be careful that you are not being misled. Verify anything you hear from a family member with other sources before accepting it completely. Don't allow yourself to be manipulated by someone with a hidden agenda.

### Ignore bad behavior

If someone attempts to disrupt the proceedings by "throwing hand grenades" at you or at another family member, ignore the first couple of instances. Not getting a reaction might be enough to disarm the troublemaker.

Reward good behavior. The other side of the coin. If someone does something positive that helps move the discussion along, reward him or her with positive feedback and sincere praise when warranted. Positive/negative reinforcement often works wonders.

### Don't ignore real issues

Contrary to the comments just above, if someone (even a troublemaker) raises a sore point more than once, you must deal with it. Repeated attempts to get an issue on the table means it is obviously important to the individual and requires airing.

### Quiet disturbers

If two or three insist on talking to each other during the discussion, distracting others and making it difficult to hear, try standing near to them as you talk. It is very hard for disturbers to keep talking to each other when the facilitator is standing right there. You also can ask them directly if they have a comment for the group (be careful with direct confrontation, however—you can turn a disturber into a real enemy and have much bigger problems).

### Restate questions and concerns

If a question is asked or a concern is raised, you may, at times, want to restate it in your own words. This will serve as a check for whether or not you fully understand the issue, and it also gives you an opportunity to state the concern without any animosity or tension directed at another individual. Use this technique to clarify the concerns minus any distracting emotional content.

### Respond to emotions

Display empathy when a concern is raised with obvious emotion behind it. "I can understand why you might feel that way" is better than "You shouldn't feel that way." Acknowledge the feelings, then restate the concern absent the feelings. Reassure the individual that you want to address the concern raised.

### Enlist helpers

If things begin to get out of hand, look to the group to quell the disturbance themselves. Someone in the family is likely to speak up and put down a disturber at some point. If there is going to be a direct confrontation with a disturber, better someone else in the family than you.

### Be prepared

In addition to knowing who the potential "problem children" are so that you can be prepared, ask the individual who clued you into the situation for ideas about how to control it. This type of family problem is not usually a new development. Many holidays and birthdays have probably witnessed the same issues being aired. Someone in the past has probably stepped up and addressed the situation. Find out what it was that seemed to work, and be prepared to use a similar technique, if necessary.

### Use tact and common sense

Don't become part of the problem by taking an overly confrontational attitude toward potential troublemakers. Remember that all family members have their own viewpoints and concerns—some are just better at expressing them than others. Sometimes, if you ignore the behavior and focus on the issue raised, tensions will decrease and permit the issue to be discussed more rationally. The Specialist, above all others, must remain cool and collected at all times.

### Use appropriate humor

Here again, if you know how to use appropriate humor effectively, it can be a terrific way to disarm a tense situation. However, the humor must be spontaneous and related to the point under discussion to be effective. Telling a joke that begins with "A guy walks into a bar..." isn't going to do it. Humor must always make a point. Humorous stories gleaned from real life, relevant to the discussion at hand, work best.

### Keep the long-term goal in mind

Your goal is to create a better tomorrow for the family and business today. Some will find the changes difficult and require time to accept it fully. Remind the audience of the long-term nature of the proposed solutions. Even if an individual doesn't get everything he or she wants right now, the long-term success of the business will provide future opportunities for them.

## Using the FBR Software

We have already discussed the FBR software and how it organizes the data collection and reporting into "Objectives desired, Objectives achieved and Objective not achieved" format. Using the software greatly simplifies the task of organizing the output.

Operating the software is very easy. It is compatible with Windows 95, Windows NT 4, and all newer Windows operating system. Once installed, you'll find the software very easy to use.

For example, on the following page, you'll find a reproduction of the input screen for entering the family's planning *Objectives*. Standard sentences appear, but they can be edited or completely replaced with your own wording. The checkboxes allow you to edit statements and determine which items will appear in the printed report.

Also on the following pages are reproductions of the screens that enable you to construct the *Suggestions* and *Conclusions* portions of the report. Again, check the appropriate boxes for the sections you want to use, and edit the output until satisfied.

The software is set up to be very user-friendly. The input sections are organized in a logical sequence:

- Introduction
- Present Plan Analysis
- Suggestions for Your Consideration
- Post-Mortem Considerations
- Conclusions
- Current Distributions Upon Death
- Proposed Distribution of Assets Upon Death
- Follow Through
- Glossary
- Print the Report

It is simply a matter of stepping through the software and selecting/editing the statements that appear. A *Go To* menu option on the upper task bar allows you to skip to a different section at any time. Note that the final option of the menu is the *Print the Report* option. This is how the final report to be used in the family retreat is created. The report uses the *Objectives Desired, Objectives Achieved* and *Objectives Not Achieved*

**FBR Report**

File   Edit   Go To.....   Help

Previous      Next

OBJECTIVES OF   Smith Family

**Personal:**
- To maintain financial security during your lives.
- To maintain flexibility during your lives.

**Family:**
- To minimize potential family conflicts.
- To treat your heirs fairly upon your demise.
- To treat your heirs equally upon your demise.

**Business:**
- To gradually turn over the operation of the business to your business heirs.
- To pass the business intact to your business heirs.
- Create a more business-like approach.

**Financial:**
- To minimize your estate taxes.
- To minimize administrative costs at death.
- To facilitate gifts to your heirs.

FBR Software: Objectives screen

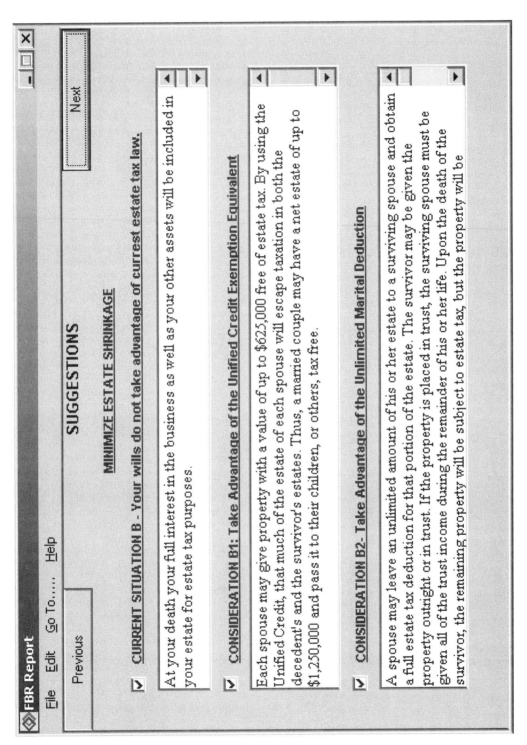

**FBR Report**

File   Edit   Go To......   Help

Previous                                    Next

## SUGGESTIONS

### MINIMIZE ESTATE SHRINKAGE

☑ <u>CURRENT SITUATION B - Your wills do not take advantage of current estate tax law.</u>

At your death your full interest in the business as well as your other assets will be included in your estate for estate tax purposes.

☑ <u>CONSIDERATION B1: Take Advantage of the Unified Credit Exemption Equivalent</u>

Each spouse may give property with a value of up to $625,000 free of estate tax. By using the Unified Credit, that much of the estate of each spouse will escape taxation in both the decedent's and the survivor's estates. Thus, a married couple may have a net estate of up to $1,250,000 and pass it to their children, or others, tax free.

☑ <u>CONSIDERATION B2- Take Advantage of the Unlimited Marital Deduction</u>

A spouse may leave an unlimited amount of his or her estate to a surviving spouse and obtain a full estate tax deduction for that portion of the estate. The survivor may be given the property outright or in trust. If the property is placed in trust, the surviving spouse must be given all of the trust income during the remainder of his or her life. Upon the death of the survivor, the remaining property will be subject to estate tax, but the property will be

FBR Software: Suggestions screen

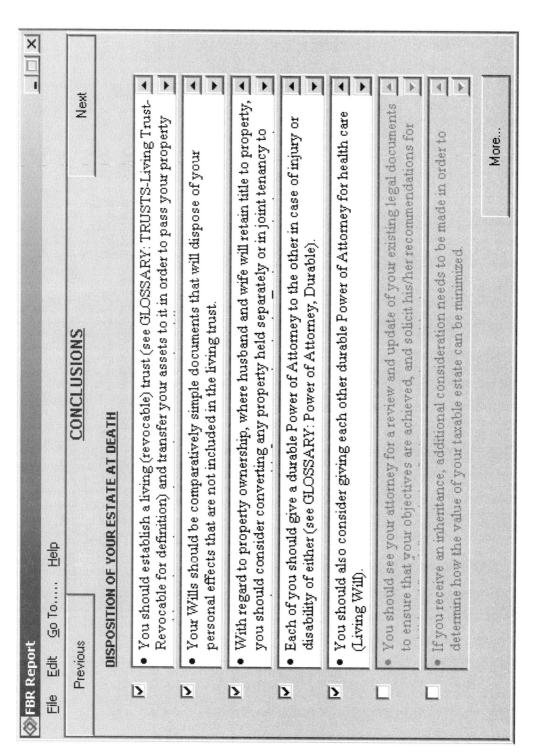

FBR Software: Conclusions screen

format. The report also contrasts the existing plan's numbers with those from the new plan.

## Marketing the Specialist

All the power of our Model is only meaningful if it is used with a sufficient number of qualified family-business owner prospects. The critical question for the Specialist is "How can I market my new skills and services effectively?" We deal with that issue next.

## Capital-intensive Businesses

The best prospects for our Model are family-owned businesses that are capital intensive—in other words, businesses that use capital and have substantial assets to pass to successors. A quick check of the yellow pages in your local telephone directory will yield a number of likely prospects. Here are some examples:

Auto Dealers and Suppliers
Banks and other Financial Institutions
Building Contractors
Dealers
Farms and Ranches
Flower Growers & Shippers
Furniture Dealers
Motel Owners
Real Estate Firms
Restaurants
Trucking Companies
Vineyards

## Third-party Trade Endorsements, Professional Alliances

One of the most effective methods of developing prospects is to actively participate in organizations that attract capital-intensive business owners.

Almost every conceivable business segment has a local state and national organization of some kind. Many were created as lobbying groups formed for the specific purpose of promoting their industry and supporting favorable legislation activity. They can be found in your local telephone book, library resources and the Internet.

There are 25 million family businesses and most belong to one or more trade associations interested in providing educational seminars for their members. Here are a few examples taken from my local yellow pages:

American Electronics
California Pork Producers
Central Coast Production Credit
Central Coast Rental Housing Owners
Central Coast Wine Growers
Certified Growers Alliance
Executives Association of San Luis Obispo
Home Builders Association of the Central Coast
International Association of Fine Art Digital Printmakers
National Electrical Contractors
San Luis Obispo Downtown
Santa Maria Valley Contractors

All trade associations that represent business owners who own plants, equipment and real estate, sell or manufacture products, are ripe with potential prospects!

To make the most of one of these organizations, join one that is a natural extension of your own interests. For example, if you were raised on a family farm and have an interest in family farming, join a local agriculture association. If you're a computer bug, perhaps an association of local computer dealers or users would be a fit.

The important point is that you involve yourself in an organization you have a natural interest or can easily establish an affinity for. Something where you already "speak the language." You should also, of course, support the goals of the organization, and be willing to volunteer whenever necessary to support the cause. You will have a serious credibility gap if you are perceived as someone who belongs to the organization strictly for self-serving reasons and no other.

Once you have identified an organization that you believe is a good fit, get involved! The best position you can hold is to be a member of the membership committee or convention planning committee. In my experience, I've been able to identify a substantial number of business owners through this type of activity. As a result, I became a life and qualifying member of the Million Dollar Round Table and a member of the Top of the Table. Working with associations put me in an excellent position to know who owned a business in the market I was interested in working in. Canvassing for new members is an excellent way to benefit an organization you believe in while introducing yourself to family business owners at the same time.

Here's how I do it. First, I approach a likely prospect for membership in the association and discuss the reasons why membership would be a good idea for them. Just before leaving, I mention my own work and ask if I might return later to explain it in more detail. I never discuss my own work without the prospect's permission, and I never short-circuit my work on behalf of the association in order to advance my own agenda.

If I'm calling on a current trade association member, I call on him or her to introduce myself as membership chairperson and ask them who else I should call on to explain the benefits of membership. Before leaving, I also mention the work I do and ask if I may come back at another time to explain it in more detail. This technique not only gets me an appointment with the current member, it also provides me names of others in the industry I can approach.

Remember your obligation to the organization. If you are the membership chairperson, concentrate on developing new members for the organization first and prospects for yourself second. You must have a sincere interest in growing the organization or this approach will fail. You will be seen as an opportunist, only interested in yourself. Once that perception develops, you're done for!

## Book for Business Owners and Family Members

To facilitate my work in the family business market, I've written a book specifically for business owners and family members entitled *Planning a Family & Business Legacy.* The purpose of the book is to introduce family business owners and family members to our Model and show them the value of a Wealth Transfer Specialist. This educational book is available as a prospecting tool. The idea is that after meeting a potential prospect, the Specialist gives him or her a copy of *Planning a Family & Business Legacy* to read. The Specialist then follows up with a personal visit to determine if the business owner is interested in pursuing the Model.

The book is designed to accomplish several objectives. First of all, it introduces the concept of the family as client, versus the business owner alone as client. It outlines our Model and details the family retreat process. The book introduces the Wealth Transfer Specialist as the individual who can facilitate the process. By the time the business owner finishes the book, he or she will have a good feel for the Model and how the family could benefit from it.

The book is written in "layman's" language and includes general information about estate and business planning issues such as death taxes and probate expenses. A glossary at the end of the book helps the reader understand unfamiliar terms.

## Wealth Transfer Educational Seminar

Another tool available to the Specialist is the FBR educational seminar. This seminar is available on 35mm slides or as a PowerPoint© presentation. It focuses on our procedure and the role of the Specialist, and is geared toward the family business owner, family members and spouses.

The goal of the seminar, like the book, is to educate and introduce the FBR Model and the Specialist. The group meeting also motivates the business owner and family members to pursue completing the Model.

The seminar materials include the presentation and script, a participant's booklet and an evaluation form designed to obtain feedback on the presentation and identify individuals interested in meeting with the Specialist. The *Planning a Family & Business Legacy* book supplements the seminar. Together, they are powerful motivators for the business owners and family members to take action.

Because the FBR Model is unique in its focus on the family as client and the family retreat, special effort must be made to introduce these new concepts to business owners and family members. The seminar and book can accomplish that task.

## Informational Family Meeting

Once a prospect is identified and interest agreed upon, the Specialist should arrange to meet with all family members and spouses as a group, along with the business owner, to describe how our Model unfolds. Again, being a unique procedure, there may be apprehension on the part of some family members. On the other hand, most family members will be excited about the prospect of a new wealth transfer plan.

The best way to approach this opportunity is to use a setting similar to the family retreat. Bring the family together and use your facilitation skills to describe how our process works and the rationale for the individual family member interviews.

The journey that the family is about to embark upon should be seen as a very positive change—one that will ultimately benefit everyone. Perhaps the evening should end with a toast to the future!

## Building Your Business as a Licensed Wealth Transfer Specialist

Becoming a licensed Specialist involves participating in special training developing and demonstrating skills. This training also includes marketing techniques and use of the FBR software and other tools. Taking advantage of additional development opportunities offered by FBR System, Inc., can result in certification as a Specialist, which carries with it additional benefits. See page 208 for an outline of our two-day training program. More information on licensing and certification can be found on the FBR System website at *www.fbrsystem.com.*

Most of this chapter focuses on getting started as a Specialist. Once you have a case or two under your belt, your personal focus must shift to growing your business. Fortunately, becoming a licensed or certified Specialist will provide you with all the tested and proven tools you'll need. Using third-party endorsements, alliances and partnerships will keep you in front of a sufficient number of excellent prospects. The workshop and business owner/family member book can help you motivate prospects into becoming your client, and the software helps streamline your ability to create a new wealth transfer plan.

The key, not surprisingly, is continuous activity. Keep the stream of prospects coming by actively working your contacts in your chosen industry. Run owner/family member educational seminars regularly and re-invite those who have declined to attend in the past. As you develop successes, the word will get out. A business owner uninterested last year may suddenly become intrigued after hearing about your work from a colleague or a competitor. Make it easy and non-threatening to attend the educational seminars—you won't regret it.

# Chapter 7 summary points:

**In this chapter we discussed:**

◈ **Developing the skills necessary to be an effective Wealth Transfer Specialist**

   **Facilitation skills**

   **Mediation skills**

   **Using the FBR software**

◈ **Tips for marketing yourself as a Specialist**

◈ **Marketing with the wealth transfer educational seminar**

◈ **Building your business as a licensed Specialist**

# Chapter 8

## Planning for Philanthropy

*If you haven't got any charity in your heart, you have the worst kind of heart trouble.*

—*Bob Hope*

Business planning of any type is usually thought of as a dry, financial transaction with no room for emotions like love and empathy. As we've seen, however, planning for the future of a family business often is fraught with emotions of all kinds. One emotion we have not considered so far, however, is benevolence or love for others outside the family.

A book about planning for the family business may seem a strange place to find a discussion of philanthropy, but as you will see, charitable giving can play a very important role in planning for the future of the family and the family business.

### Why Philanthropy?

We've seen how planning for the continuation of the family business is a way of leaving a legacy for the future. Leaving behind a thriving business for the benefit of your family, and your employees and their families, is a very worthwhile objective. Including charitable giving in your planning provides a way to leave a second legacy—to your community and perhaps the world.

Philanthropy accomplishes a number of things. It provides you with the satisfaction of helping others, for one. Generosity has its own rewards in that regard. Serving as a model of generosity for your children, grandchildren and other family members also has its rewards. Involving the family in the operation of a family charitable foundation or a donor-advised fund is a tremendously satisfying way to instill charitable motives in other family members.

Another very important benefit of charitable giving is financial—in the form of tax savings and incentives. Sometimes, including charitable gifting in business planning results in substantial financial gain over other planning techniques. In fact, one business owner I worked with viewed charitable giving as strictly a financial transaction.

Let's call him Larry. Larry felt strongly that, at his death, none of his wealth should go to the government in the form of estate taxes. Having been a bachelor all his life, Larry decided to make gifts of part of his business interest to his heirs—23 nieces and nephews. The balance of his estate—over $350,000—went to a number of charities. The choice of charities was not important to him. He merely wanted to redirect his assets from the government to charity—any charity. Of course, the charities were happy to receive the money regardless of Larry's motivation.

While Larry was somewhat unusual in that his philanthropy was motivated entirely by financial desires rather than altruism, his approach does underscore the power of charitable giving as a financial planning tool.

These two features, the ability to leave a second legacy, and the tax benefits for the family are all powerful motivators for including philanthropy in family business planning. While every family will not be interested in charitable planning, be sure to discuss this issue so your client becomes aware of its many emotional and financial benefits. Also, it will help distinguish you from your competition because few business advisors understand the many benefits of charitable planning and fewer still discuss it with their clients.

## The Charitable Buy-Sell Arrangement.

One arrangement that combines business planning with philanthropy is called the charitable buy-sell. Here's how it works.

Suppose Mary owns 90 percent of a business and her son Andy owns the remaining 10 percent. Andy wants to own the entire business at some point, and Mary would like to spend her retirement years helping her alma mater—her favorite charity.

Mary and Andy enter into a formal buy-sell agreement with the usual terms controlling the disposition of the stock in the corporation when Mary dies. According to the agreement, at Mary's death, Andy must purchase the stock from her estate, and the estate is obligated to sell it.

Each year, Mary makes gifts of some of her corporate stock to her alma mater. Let's assume the value of the gift is $150,000 each year. If we further assume Mary's current tax rate is 35 percent, her donation will generate $52,500 in tax savings. Mary can then make a gift to Andy of a portion of the tax savings to fund the premiums on life insurance on her life. When Mary dies, the life insurance proceeds will be used by Andy to make the stock purchase.

In the meantime, Mary's alma mater does not want to hold on to a minority interest in Mary and Andy's business, so it attempts to sell the stock each year. Obviously, the only realistic potential buyer is Andy or the corporation itself. Ideally, excess earnings in the corporation can be used to redeem the stock from the university each year.

The results can be impressive! The university receives $150,000 per year (in cash after the stock is sold), Mary receives a substantial tax deduction, and Andy increases his percentage of business ownership during his lifetime and knows he can complete the purchase of the corporate stock at Mary's death because of the funded buy-sell agreement. Everyone wins!

Of course, to make a plan like this work it must be very carefully designed. The university cannot be required to sell the stock and the corporation cannot be legally obligated to buy it. The value of the stock must also be determined very carefully to pass IRS muster. Nevertheless, the charitable buy-sell arrangement can be a very useful tool for someone

interested in passing the family business to the next generation and benefiting a charity in the process.

## Charitable Family Limited Partnership

This is a somewhat more complex approach to philanthropic business
planning.

In this case, the family creates a family limited partnership with the
current owner or owners serving as the general partner(s). The general
partners manage the affairs of the partnership while the limited partners
have no voice in its operation. The general partners control the partnership even though they might own only one percent of the partnership
while the limited partners own 99 percent. The assets of the partnership
consist of the family business interest.

All or a portion of the limited partnership interest is transferred immediately, or over time, to a charity. Based on the value of the partnership
interests donated, the donors receive an income tax deduction. In addition, the amount of the gift is removed from their taxable estate at death,
saving potential estate taxes. The charity receives its proportionate share
of the income generated by the partnership. At the end of the partnership
time period, say 50 years, the partnership expires, assets are sold and the
charity receives its share of the sale. In the meantime, the charity may also
have the right to liquidate its share of the limited partnership before the
time period expires.

Here again, the charitable family limited partnership must be very carefully structured. This arrangement can result in taxable income for the
charity, which may be objectionable, and the right to liquidate may pose
a problem for the charity if not carefully structured.

The benefits of the charitable family limited partnership are many. The
charity receives an income stream for a period of years and a lump sum
payout at the end of the partnership period, the current owners receive
an income tax deduction and reduce their taxable estate. Eventually,
the partnership period expires and the business is sold—perhaps to the
family members living at that time. In the meantime, family members

can be employed by the business and receive a management fee for managing the family limited partnership. In addition, the family maintains control of the business during the partnership period.

## Charitable Remainder Trust

The charitable remainder trust (CRT) is another tool that can be used in family business planning.

A CRT is a trust with only charities as beneficiaries. Property transferred to a CRT is considered a gift to charity and can potentially provide three types of tax savings. First of all, the gift generates an income tax deduction for the donor. Secondly, if the property is subject to capital gains taxes (farmland purchased long ago, for example) the capital gains tax is avoided. Thirdly, the gift to the CRT reduces the donor's taxable estate, thereby reducing estate taxes.

The other attractive feature of a CRT is that it pays income to the creator of the trust (or someone designated by him or her) for life or for a set number of years. At the end of the payout period, the balance of the funds in the trust belongs to the charity. A CRT is ideal for someone with appreciated assets who desires income, wants to benefit a charity or charities and also save taxes in the process.

The one drawback to a CRT is that the charity must wait until the end of the payout period to realize its gift.

## Charitable Lead Trust

The charitable lead trust (CLT) can be thought of as the polar opposite of the CRT described above.

In the CLT, property is placed into a charitable trust and the income is paid to the charity for a set number of years. At the end of the period, the property reverts back to the donor. This arrangement works for an individual with income-producing property who doesn't need the income for a period of time and wishes to benefit a charity or charities.

The donor receives a tax deduction for the value of the income given to the charity. Estate taxes can be saved to the extent that the earnings directed to the charity do not increase the estate's value.

Both the CRT and the CLT are subject to various rules, but neither is difficult to establish nor costly to manage. Both are excellent tools for benefiting charities while providing important tax benefits to the donor and his or her family.

## Private Foundations

A private foundation is an arrangement whereby a board of directors manages funds for the benefit of charities it chooses. There are many private foundations still in existence that were created long ago by wealthy families. Names like Ford, Carnegie and Melon come to mind. Fortunately, you do not have to have that level of wealth to create and manage a family charitable foundation. Many times they can be set up in conjunction with a community foundation greatly reducing the set up and operating costs.

A major attraction to the family foundation is its potential for teaching philanthropy to succeeding generations of family members. Usually, the board of directors is made up of family members who meet periodically to choose the charities and amounts to be awarded. This process can be an extremely rewarding exercise for the family. It can include visiting the charities, interviewing its managers, and researching its goals and operating successes. The experience offers a first-hand opportunity to see the charity in operation and learn about its mission.

Obviously, the funds for the family foundation must come from somewhere. The proceeds from a lifetime sale of a business interest could be a source. Using the proceeds from a sale at the death of an owner is another possibility.

A very attractive feature of the private foundation is that it can use the family name in its title. Think of the satisfaction your client would have in knowing that long after his or her death, the community would still be receiving benefits from the "Smith Family Foundation" and members of the Smith family would still be on the board, choosing beneficiaries and directing its operations. This is an example of leaving two legacies—a successful business for the family and employees, and a charitable foundation for the community.

## Donor Advised Fund

A donor advised fund (DAF) has some of the same characteristics as the private foundation, but is lower in cost and not quite as flexible.

A DAF is basically a fund operated for the benefit of charities. The donor receives tax advantages by making contributions to the fund and can "advise" the fund as to which charities to benefit, but cannot force the DAF to honor those particular charities. As a practical matter, however, the DAF usually will honor the donor's "advice" since to do otherwise would discourage future donations.

The DAF has the advantage of being very simple and cost effective. The family can serve as an informal "board of directors" for the charities it advises, similar to the private foundation. The DAF will not carry the family name, however.

Although it is less formal than the family foundation, the DAF still accomplishes a lot of good and permits teaching philanthropy to succeeding family generations.

Again, the funds for the DAF donation can come from the business and estate planning efforts.

## Conclusion

From this brief discussion, hopefully you can see how including philanthropy in family business and estate planning offers many benefits. The satisfaction of helping a church, school or university, or other charitable causes and institutions while modeling philanthropy for others in the family are reasons enough for families to choose this type of planning. Substantial tax benefits are another compelling reason.

The focus of much of this book has been on leaving the family business to succeeding generations as a legacy rather than a tragedy. Including philanthropy in family business planning provides the opportunity to leave a second legacy—one that can benefit favorite charitable institutions long after the current business owners are gone. Think about the appeal of that!

Discuss charitable planning with your family-business clients. You can accomplish a lot of good in your community and provide a rewarding planning experience for your clients as well. And remember, you set yourself apart from other business advisors because very few of them include charitable planning in their work with clients. Think of it as a way you can leave your own personal legacy to your community!

The next two chapters are a review of the fundamentals of business transfer and estate planning. If you already are familiar with this information, you might want to skip or merely skim the material. On the other hand, if these concepts are new to you, you should be able to gain a basic understanding of these topics by studying the next two chapters.

An in-depth study of technical topics is beyond the scope of this book. An excellent source of in-depth content are the study courses offered by the American College of Bryn Mawr, PA through the Chartered Life Underwriter (CLU), Chartered Financial Consultant (ChFC) and Certified Financial Planner (CFP) courses of study. Attorneys, accountants and other business advisors have designations and specialties also. The LLM degree for attorneys, for example, indicates special education in taxation.

Review the following two chapters as needed. Good luck to you in your career as a Wealth Transfer Specialist!

# Chapter 8 summary points:

In this chapter we discussed:

❖ Philanthropy in business planning offers many benefits for the business, the family and the community

❖ Various tools and techniques are available for charitable planning

The Charitable Buy-Sell Arrangement.

Charitable Family Limited Partnership

Charitable Remainder Trust

Charitable Lead Trust

Private Foundations

Donor Advised Fund

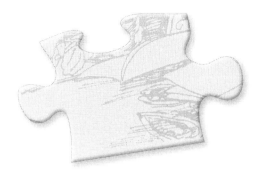

# Chapter 9

## Fundamentals of Business Succession Planning

*If a man empties his purse into his head, no man can take it away from him. An investment in knowledge always pays the best interest.*

—*Benjamin Franklin*

In this chapter we will take a closer look at various aspects of planning for the continuation of a business. This should not be taken as an in-depth treatment of the subject. If you are not versed in business succession planning, this material will give you some background and a basic understanding of the subject.

### Business Organizations

Most businesses are organized in one of three basic structures—although there are a number of others that are becoming more popular. We'll touch on the most common.

### *Sole Proprietorship*

The sole proprietorship is the simplest and most basic form of business structure. Many businesses begin as sole proprietorships and change to another form at some point for tax or other reasons.

Becoming a sole proprietor is easy. You basically hang out a shingle and announce to the world that you are in business. Generally speaking, the sole proprietor need only be concerned with issues like licensing, local building and selling codes and a few other issues related to the business to be conducted before throwing open the doors.

The sole proprietorship also is uncomplicated from a tax perspective. There is no distinction between the individual as a taxpayer and the business. Although the sole proprietor may keep separate books on business activity and use a business checking account for business related finances, all money earned by the business is considered personal income to the sole proprietor and taxed accordingly. The simple structure of the sole proprietorship is one of its attractions.

The sole proprietorship also has a significant disadvantage, however. All debts incurred by the business are personal debts. All business liabilities are personal liabilities. That means if someone sues the sole proprietor and wins, they might walk off with the owner's house, car and everything else he or she owns. The lack of protection from business liability is one of the main reasons sole proprietors eventually abandon this form of doing business.

### Partnership

The simplest way to view a partnership is to think of it as two or more sole proprietors in business together. Everything said above about the sole proprietor regarding taxation and liability are true of partners in a general partnership as well. In addition, there is another danger in being a partner. Any general partner can obligate the partnership and make all the individual partners liable for anything that goes wrong. Obviously, an individual should choose his or her partners carefully.

Partnerships usually are formed because two individuals complement each other in skills, expertise or other requirement of a business. Partners split the income in the partnership based on the terms of their agreement. Just like sole proprietors, once income is earned, it's taxed to the partners—even if that income is "plowed back into the business." The personal liability issue is again a primary motivator in switching from the partnership form of business to a different form.

### *Corporation*

A corporation is a legal entity separate from its owners. It is considered in many respects to be a citizen. Like its human counterpart, the corporation can own property in its name, sue others and be sued. In fact, a corporation can do almost anything a human citizen can do, except vote. The biggest distinction between the corporate form of business and all others, in addition to the things just mentioned, is the liability protection it affords its owners.

If you own stock in any company, you are an owner. If the company or the company product harms someone and is sued, however, you are liable only up to the value of your stock. In other words, if your corporation loses a lawsuit, the winner cannot take your house and other personal belongings. The worst that could happen is the stock you own could become worthless. This is true whether you own stock in IBM or Jack's Hardware, Inc. It's also true if you own one share of stock or all the outstanding stock of a corporation.

When a small business incorporates, the owners have the advantage of the limited liability, unless the owner does something that allows a litigant to "pierce the corporate veil." An example of this might be an incorporated business where the operator conceals the fact that the business is a corporation. Customers and vendors have the right to know they are dealing with a corporation if, indeed, that is the case. If Jack conducts his hardware business in a manner that conceals the fact it is a corporation, a dissatisfied customer might be successful in suing Jack personally—circumventing the protection otherwise afforded by incorporation.

The other big distinction of the corporation is that it is taxed separately from its owners. This has a good and bad side to it. Paying additional tax is not generally an advantage, but small businesses often are taxed at a rate lower than their owner's personal tax rate. This means that if the owner can use corporate funds to pay for personal benefits, he or she will save money by paying for the benefit with lower taxed dollars. Having the corporation lease a car or pay the owner's life insurance premiums are examples of using corporate dollars for personal benefits. Of course there are rules about all this, so it isn't as easy as simply writing a check from the corporate checkbook. Accounting for personal use of business assets can be very complicated.

The bad news side of being incorporated is that it is sometimes difficult to get money out of a successful corporation. If a corporation has profits beyond a certain amount, it is supposed to pay those profits to the owners in the form of a dividend. Dividend payments are not deductible to the corporation, but they are taxable to the recipient. This means that owners of family corporations are loath to pay dividends, preferring to receive corporate dollars as deductible compensation instead. Here again, things can get complicated. If you own a corporation and "over pay" yourself in an effort to avoid paying dividends, you may run into the "unreasonable compensation" rules in the Internal Revenue Code. These rules are in place to prevent just that and force corporations to pay dividends instead of salaries in some cases.

### S Corporation

An "S Corporation" is, in essence, a corporation that is taxed like a partnership. That means the owners have the limited liability of a corporate owner, but the single-tax structure of a sole proprietorship or partnership. This "best of both worlds" is an attempt to take advantage of the best features of both types of business organization. As with everything else, there are limitations and drawbacks to S Corporation status. For example, S Corporations are limited in the number and types of owners they can have and the types of stock they offer owners. There are other limitations as well that sometimes makes this business structure less desirable. Accounting for S corporations is complicated.

Many times a new business will start out as an S Corporation because it is expected to lose money for the first few years, and the investors want to be able to take advantage of those losses the way a partner or sole proprietor can. As the business grows and becomes profitable, the company might later switch to C or "regular" corporation status.

### Limited Liability Company

This is a relatively newer form of business organization. The LLC can elect to be taxed like either a partnership or a corporation. Most companies that elect LLC status do so in order to take advantage of the limited liability. An LLC, while similar in many respects to an S Corporation, is simpler and involves fewer restrictions. LLC owners are referred to as "members."

The one disadvantage of the LLC is that it is a newer form of business structure and there is some inconsistency among the various states and, as a result, some uncertainty. Nevertheless, it is becoming increasingly popular as a business form.

### Limited Partnership

A limited partnership is one where some of the partners have liability protection similar to that of a corporation or LLC. These individuals are referred to as "limited partners." They have an investment in the business, but are not actively engaged in its operation. One or more general partners conduct the business. If the partnership runs into trouble—is sued, for example—only the general partners are personally liable. The worst that can happen to the limited partners is that they could lose their investment.

A variation of this organizational structure is called the family limited partnership. This is a limited partnership formed by a family usually for purposes of transferring a portion of a business interest to other family members. Using the limited partnership method sometimes results in significant income and estate tax savings, and permits moving some of the business ownership to other family members while protecting the current owner's control of the business.

## The Big Picture

Every business will someday face a transition. This could range all the way from liquidation to outright sale. The key to business planning is to make sure that when the transition happens, it is orderly and results in the preservation of as much of the owner's wealth as possible. Let's review the various strategies.

### Liquidation

Although not usually thought of as a business strategy, liquidation is nevertheless the fate of many small businesses. Many times it is the best alternative. A good example is the "one-person shop" type of business. If Susan operates a one person bookkeeping business, for example, the business may only exist for as long as Susan is there keeping books. When Susan walks out, for whatever reason, the business ceases to exist for all practical purposes.

Businesses like Susan's often are sole proprietorships. If there is no family member or key employee who wants to take over Susan's business when she dies or retires, liquidation may be a good alternative. A book-keeping business usually does not have a lot in the way of assets. Nevertheless, it can be quite valuable to the family. Suppose Susan makes $75,000 per year at her business. To the family, that is the equivalent of having $750,000 in an investment earning 10 percent interest. If Susan dies, however, her computer, desk and file cabinets might bring the family only a fraction of that. Selling her business files to another accounting business might generate a bit more, but there is no way to get $750,000 from the sale of Susan's assets.

One way Susan can make sure her family receives the full value of the business if she dies is to insure her life for the difference between the "book value" of the business and its value as a going concern. In this case, if we assume Susan's assets could bring $100,000, we could insure her life for $650,000 which would assure the family that if Susan died unexpectedly, the family would have a sum of money to invest to replace her lost income.

### *Sale as a going concern*

Suppose instead of a bookkeeping business, Susan owns a profitable business making and selling widgets. Any number of individuals might like to buy that business if Susan dies or decides to retire. Another member of the family—her son, for instance, could be a potential buyer. Maybe a competitor or a key employee would be interested in buying it.

Regardless of who is interested in buying the business, the mechanics of the buy-out plan would be the same. Generally, a buy-sell agreement would be the preferred solution.

### *Cross Purchase*

A buy-sell agreement is a legally binding arrangement between Susan and the buyer. If the buyer is a partner or co-stockholder of Susan, the arrangement is called a "cross-purchase" agreement. In essence, each person agrees to buy the business interest from the other's estate if one of the owners dies. The buy-out might also be triggered by a disability or lifetime sale as well. The most effective funding mechanism for a buy-sell agreement is life and/or disability insurance. That way, if the death or disability of an owner occurs, the money automatically is available to execute the buy-sell agreement. Installment payments and side funds are also sometimes used alone or in combination with insurance to fund the plan.

### *Stock Redemption/Entity Agreement*

Sometimes, in the case of a corporation or partnership, the preferred arrangement is to have the business itself buy the stock or business interest if an owner dies, retires or becomes disabled. This form of buy-sell is called a stock redemption plan if the business is a corporation and an entity plan if the business is a partnership. It works essentially the same way as a cross-purchase arrangement. If an owner dies, the business redeems the business interest by purchasing it from the decedent's estate. Funding is similar to the cross-purchase arrangement, except in this case, the business would own the insurance or other funding vehicle.

In either case—cross-purchase or entity buy-sell—the result is the same. At the end of the buy-sell transaction, the deceased business owner's estate holds cash instead of a non-liquid business interest.

### Wait and See buy-sell

Often, it is difficult for a family to decide if a buy-sell arrangement should be set up as cross-purchase or stock redemption/entity. After all, all the facts surrounding the sale and purchase won't be clear until an owner actually dies. One remedy for this dilemma is called the "Wait and See Buy-sell."

The Wait and See Buy-sell provides maximum flexibility. It provides that if an owner dies, the corporation has the option to purchase the business interest (redemption/entity). If the business doesn't purchase it, the other owners may buy it (cross-purchase). If the owners don't purchase the business interest, then the business must purchase it. This third element, the required purchase by the company if the co-owners do not purchase, is what makes this a binding buy-sell agreement.

The Wait and See Buy-sell is increasingly popular as a planning tool because of its flexibility.

### Key Person Buy-out

In some cases, the best prospect for a buy-out is a key employee. If no family member were interested in buying the business at the death or retirement of the current owner, perhaps a key employee would like to purchase it. If that's the case, an agreement is made between the current owner and the key employee that works just like the other buy-sell arrangements described. The key person usually owns life insurance on the current owner. When the owner dies, the key person uses the death proceeds to purchase the business interest from the deceased owner's estate. Installment payments, loans and other investments also can be part of the funding arrangement.

### Trusteed Agreements

Any of the buy-sell arrangements described above can be structured using a trustee to execute the agreement when the time comes. This is sometimes desirable because it introduces a disinterested third party into the arrangement, assuring impartiality. When this arrangement is used, the trustee usually holds the life insurance policies or other funding vehicles and is responsible for executing the plan as set down in the terms of the trust.

### Charitable Buy-sell

If the owners are charitably inclined, a buy-sell can be structured in a way that benefits a charity or charitable trust. The current owner simply names a charity or charitable trust as beneficiary of the business interest at death. Because the charity does not want to operate a business, it hopes to sell the business interest quickly. The most likely buyers are family members interested in owning the business. The family members purchase the business interest from the charity or trust. The sale price may be discounted because it is a minority interest with a limited market.

The result is that the surviving family members receive the business interest at a bargain price, and the charity receives cash. The estate of the deceased owner receives a charitable deduction, reducing estate tax liability.

A charitable buy-sell can be a valuable planning tool, but it can be very difficult to structure in a way that meets all IRS requirements for charitable income and estate taxes. Nevertheless, owners with a philanthropic bent may be attracted to such an arrangement.

### Private Life Annuity

In many cases, it makes sense for the next generation of owners to buy out the current owners on the installment plan. This usually means transferring ownership of the business to the next generation and taking money from the business operation and using it to make installment payments. The payments typically last until the terms of the purchase are met. If the current owner dies during the buy-out, payments typically continue to the decedent's estate.

A variation of the installment plan is called the private life annuity. It is similar to installment payments except that the duration of the payments lasts until the current owner or owners die. That means the total of all payments may be more or less than a pure installment purchase. The value of it is that the sellers have the security of a lifetime income.

One business I worked with had a son who had been managing the family business for some 20 years but did not own any interest in the business. When I met the family, everyone seemed to feel he was entitled to own the business, but the parents had never made any arrangements to pass the business to him. The stumbling block was the other five children in the family. The parents were concerned about treating them all fairly.

After consulting with the family members and their trusted advisors, it was determined that a life annuity buy-out by the son had more favorable income tax consequences than an installment sale. The attorney drafted the necessary documents to put the plan into effect. In addition to the tax advantages, the life annuity accomplished two other very important goals; it assured the parents of receiving retirement income for life, and it passed ownership of the business immediately to the managing son. The other children in the family also benefited from the arrangement because they stood to inherit cash and other assets from their parent's estate instead of becoming co-owners in the family business with their brother.

## Key employees

Another important consideration when planning for the long-term success of a business is the key employees that contribute to its success. If the goal is to keep the business operating profitably, it is usually a good idea to tie the key employees tightly to the business. This can be done in a variety of ways through the use of employee benefits or "perks." Some are referred to as "golden handcuffs" because they make it difficult for the employee to leave. These can take the form of bonuses, stock options or other incentives.

Some common tools for benefiting key employees are deferred compensation, salary continuation, split-dollar life insurance and group health and life insurance. Because many employee benefits have non-discrimination rules attached to them, it sometimes is difficult to craft a plan that favors key people over rank-and-file employees. Nevertheless, a number of these—such as salary continuation and split-dollar life insurance—are very attractive fringe benefits because discrimination is allowed.

### Salary Continuation

This is an agreement between the business and a key employee that provides for continued salary for the key person at retirement, disability or some other triggering event. The salary continuation usually is subject to forfeiture if the key employee leaves the employer or fails to meet some other requirement. The forfeiture provisions can be almost anything. Non-compete clauses are common, as are requirements to serve as a consultant after retirement.

The attractiveness of salary continuation is that the employee has a very nice benefit to look forward to, and the employer has assurance the employee will remain loyal and continue to help the business remain profitable.

### Split-dollar Life Insurance

Key employees, like virtually everyone else, have needs for life insurance protection for their family. Employers can help pay the cost of this insurance through the use of a technique called "split-dollar." Split-dollar allows the employer to pay the premiums for a key person's personal life insurance without the premium amount becoming taxable as compensation to the employee. A full description of split-dollar is beyond the scope of this book, but suffice it to say, it can be an attractive example of the golden handcuffs.

### *Section 162 Bonus Plan*

This is another means of paying for a key employee's insurance. In this case, however, the benefit is not limited to life insurance. Long-term care insurance, disability insurance, even annuities can be paid for by the employer using this technique. In essence, the employer pays the premium for the employee's insurance or annuity and adds the dollar amount to the employee's W-2 form as additional compensation. Since the additional compensation causes the employee to pay additional tax, the employer also can add a cash bonus to the plan to cover the additional tax. Section 162 plans (named for the IRC section that enables them) are very simple yet offer attractive benefits for key employees.

Key employee perks can be an important part of planning for business transition because of their importance to the continued success of the operation. If an owner dies or retires, key people may not have the same level of confidence in the new owners as they did with the previous owner. As a result, they may be tempted to leave and pursue other opportunities. Key person perks can make sure that doesn't happen.

In addition to perks for the key people, businesses may also own "key-person insurance." This is life or disability insurance on the lives of key employees that reimburses the business if the key person dies or becomes disabled and unable to work. The purpose of key-person insurance is to protect the business from the premature loss of a key employee. In many family businesses, various family members are key people and are covered by key-person insurance.

## Estate Coordination

The next chapter deals with estate planning matters. It's worth mentioning here that business and estate planning go hand in hand. They are opposite sides of the same planning coin.

Often business and estate planning are treated as two separate processes that can be pursued independently. In those cases, it is easy to develop an estate plan that defeats the business plan, or vice-versa. For example, if your estate plan calls for leaving estate assets equally to your children, but your business plan calls for one daughter to succeed you as principle owner, there likely will be a conflict.

Always remember that at death, the very first person in line with his hand out is Uncle Sam. Taxes are the first consideration when it comes to finalizing estate settlement. If tax requirements mean the loss of the business, so be it. If you have any doubts this is true, study the many examples of famous estates. Bing Crosby had to buy his own assets back from the estate of his deceased wife, Dixie. John Wayne's son lost his father's ranch and cattle feeding operation because of the lack of estate planning. The Robbie family was forced to sell part of the Miami Dolphins to pay taxes at the death of Joe Robbie. There are countless other examples.

## Conclusion

Business owners are in a very enviable position in many respects. People often wish they had the power and freedom that come with owning their own business—not realizing the amount of sacrifice involved. Business owners are often seen as lucky because they control their own destiny to a large extent.

With the advantages of business ownership, however, come a number of difficult decisions—not the least of which is "how should the business ultimately be transferred and to whom?" There are many tools available to the business owner to facilitate ownership transfer—some have been discussed here. The key concept to keep in mind is that transfer techniques are usually complex and must be evaluated carefully. The counsel of trusted advisors is imperative. And, most of all, remember there is simply no substitute for careful planning.

# Chapter 9 summary points:

In this chapter we discussed the fundamentals of business succession planning:

❖ **Types of business organizations**

   Sole proprietorships

   Partnerships

   Corporations

   Other business organizations

❖ **Methods of transferring business ownership**

❖ **Benefits for key employees**

❖ **Coordinating business planning with estate planning**

# Chapter 10

## Fundamentals of Estate Planning

*Two weeks of solid work on his estate may be worth more to an executive than his financial gains of the past ten to fifteen years.*

*—Joseph D. Coughlan, "Executive Blindspot,"*
*Price Waterhouse Review, Autumn 1966*

Estate planning is another one of those complex subjects that is more properly the subject of an entire book than a chapter. Regardless, we'll take it on by treating the subject with a broad brush, providing at least a basic understanding of the more important considerations.

### The Estate Tax

The estate tax we will be concerned with is a federal tax on the right to pass property to others upon one's death. Some states also have an estate tax, but they will not be addressed here. In addition, some states have an inheritance tax, which is a tax on an individual's right to receive property from a decedent. Likewise, inheritance taxes will not be addressed here. Together, these taxes are sometimes referred to "death taxes."

As this is being written, the Economic Growth and Tax Relief Reconciliation Act of 2001 (EGTRRA) has greatly affected the estate planning landscape. Basically, EGTRRA reduces the effect of the estate tax and eventually fully repeals it. As things currently stand, if you die in 2010, you will owe no federal estate tax. Die in 2011, however, and only $1 million escapes taxation. This is due to the fact that EGTRRA contains a ten-year "sunset" provision, meaning the law goes away ten years after it is enacted.

Planning for a one-year repeal is awkward. However, there is much uncertainty around this issue and changes in the law over the next few years is almost certain. For our purposes, we will deal with the federal estate tax law as it currently stands. You must rely on your advisors to deal with the ambiguity of the current situation.

## Estate Basics

There are a number of issues around estate taxes that easily cause confusion. For one thing, the "estate" for federal estate tax purposes is often confused with the "estate" for probate purposes. These are two entirely separate things. Your probate estate consists of all the property that passes to heirs through your will or through state intestacy laws if you have no will. Because a will is a public document and probate involves some expense, individuals often structure property ownership to avoid probate. Owning property jointly with right of survivorship, for example, allows property to pass from a deceased owner to the surviving joint owner without passing through probate. This type of planning can be useful, but it may not have any effect on the federal estate taxes due.

Estate planning concerns itself with positioning assets and using various planning techniques to minimize the amount of estate tax due at death. This process also may reduce the probate estate, but this is not the primary goal.

Simply put, your estate consists of everything you own at the time of your death. That includes property in all forms such as real estate; intangible assets like stocks, bonds and life insurance; and personal property like cars, jewelry and cash. The trick to reducing federal estate taxes is to reduce the size of your estate at your death. Easier said than done—especially for the family business owner.

### The Estate Tax

The federal estate tax is calculated as a percentage of the assets you own at your death. Spouses have an unlimited marital deduction for property passed between them at death. Utilizing the marital deduction, a married couple incurs no estate tax at the death of the first spouse, but can experience a substantial tax at the second death. Proper planning can reduce or even eliminate the tax at the second death. More about that later.

The amount of property sheltered from the estate tax depends upon the tax credit available. The credit translates into a dollar value of property exempt from taxation. The chart below shows the property exemption amounts and the top tax rates currently included in the law.

| Year | Top Estate Tax Rate | Applicable Exclusion Amount |
|---|---|---|
| 2002 | 50% | $1,000,000 |
| 2003 | 49% | $1,000,000 |
| 2004 | 48% | $1,500,000 |
| 2005 | 47% | $1,500,000 |
| 2006 | 46% | $2,000,000 |
| 2007 | 45% | $2,000,000 |
| 2008 | 45% | $2,000,000 |
| 2009 | 45% | $3,500,000 |
| 2010 | *Zero tax; estate tax repealed for one year* | |
| 2011 | 50% | $1,000,000 |

Based on this schedule, if you die in 2008, $2 million of your estate will escape taxation. The balance will be taxed on a sliding scale, with the highest tax rate being 45 percent. If you are so fortunate as to die in 2010, no tax is due. Live another year, however, and you will have only $1 million of property escape taxation. Again, legislation between now and 2011 undoubtedly will change this picture. Whether it will be better or worse remains to be seen.

## Estate Tax Issues

Given that the federal estate tax rates are so high, it is definitely worthwhile to plan your affairs so as to minimize the amount of property subject to the tax. Regardless of how you feel about paying taxes, you are under no obligation to pay the maximum. Avoiding estate taxes is a legitimate goal for estate planning. Evading taxes, of course, is illegal. Competent estate tax advisors plan for reducing the taxation as much as possible by taking advantage of the provisions within the law.

There are a number of ways to reduce the taxation. Generally they involve the use of trusts and various types of property ownership to accomplish this goal. Let's briefly review some of the possibilities.

## Trusts

If you give property to a trust, you no longer own it. The trust owns it and holds it for the benefit of the beneficiaries of the trust. If you are both trustee and beneficiary of a trust, you have not removed the trust assets from your estate. In effect, you still own it because you have complete control of it.

One of the most common types of trust is the so-called bypass or credit shelter trust. This trust is designed to take advantage of the exemption available to the first spouse, rather than allowing it to be wasted. The chart below shows an example contrasting a simple will (everything to spouse at the first death, everything to children at the second death) with a bypass trust strategy. The example assumes a $2.5 million total estate and death in 2002.

Note that there is no tax on the first death, but a $680,000 estate tax due at the second death. This is the effect of the unlimited marital deduction. No tax is due on property left to a spouse (who is a U.S. citizen) regardless of the dollar amount. Unfortunately, the $1 million exclusion the first spouse could have taken advantage of is wasted because the second spouse is only entitled to a single $1 million exclusion when passing assets to the children. The second chart shows how a trust could help the situation.

## Simple Will

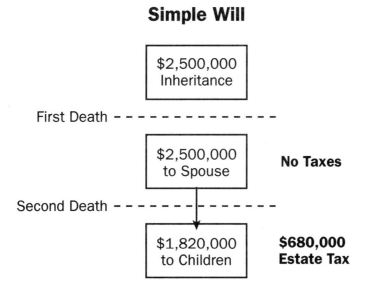

**Total to children = $1,820,000**

In this scenario, $1.5 million is left directly to the surviving spouse at the death of the first spouse; and $1 million, the amount of the exclusion, is placed in a trust. The surviving spouse gets the income from the trust and has the ability to withdraw a limited amount of the principal.

## Bypass Trust Will

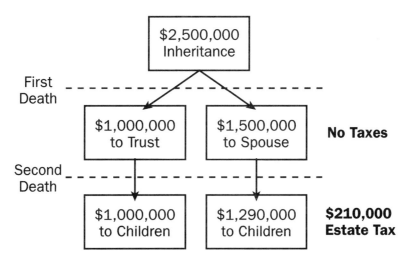

**Total to children = $2,290,000**

Many people are reluctant to visit an attorney for fear of having to pay fees for legal work. I don't think there is an attorney anywhere in the country that would charge $470,000 to include a bypass trust in an individual's will!

Creating a will with the bypass trust feature is probably the most common estate planning technique. The same thing can be accomplished using a revocable living trust in place of a will. The operation is identical, but the revocable trust takes the place of the will. Revocable trusts are popular because they are, as the name implies, revocable or changeable like a will, but unlike a will, they are not public documents.

### Property ownership

Depending upon the state involved, property owned by spouses may or may not be considered completely their own. In most states, property ownership is straightforward. If your name is on the title of a car, for example, it is your property. However, ten states use community property as the standard—meaning virtually everything owned by either spouse, in effect, belongs one-half to each of them. There are some exceptions to this rule in community property states, but generally speaking, if you live in Arizona, California, Idaho, Louisiana, Nevada, New Mexico, Texas, Washington or Wisconsin, half of just about everything you own belongs to your spouse. In Alaska, married couples have the option to elect community property treatment of assets.

The problem with community property is that it can make it difficult to reposition ownership of assets in order to properly fund a bypass trust and take full advantage of the available exemption. In non-community property states, it is relatively easy to move ownership of some assets from one spouse to the other. It is important to coordinate property ownership with the provisions of one's will; and equalizing estate asset ownership is sometimes a key to taking full advantage of all the available estate tax credits.

### *Carryover basis*

Under current law, when an individual dies, generally property he or she owns is "stepped up" in value to its fair market value on the date of death. Heirs inherit the property at this stepped-up value. For example, if an individual purchased farm land years ago for $1,000 per acre, but the land is now worth $2,500 per acre, selling the land ordinarily triggers a capital gains tax on the $1,500 gain. If the individual dies, however, the heirs inherit the land with a $2,500 per acre cost basis. That means if an heir subsequently sells the property, he or she will only pay capital gains tax on anything received over $2,500 per acre. The gain from $1,000 per acre to $2,500 per acre goes untaxed.

EGTRRA will change that, if the law remains in place as is. Beginning in 2010, the stepped-up basis rule is modified. The first $1.3 million of estate assets are treated as under the existing rule. In addition, $3 million left to a surviving spouse receives the stepped-up value. The balance of the estate property passes to heirs with the decedent's basis intact. That means the decedent must keep detailed records of the amounts paid for assets, and the heirs must have access to that information. Again, all this could change drastically between now and 2010—stay tuned.

### *Gifts*

Another very effective way to reduce the value of your taxable estate is to give it away before you die. Gifts are a very effective means of reducing the taxable estate and a common planning tool. Of course, the downside to making a gift is that the asset is no longer yours. When giving away portions of a business interest, one has to be careful that one doesn't give away controlling interest in the business. Nevertheless, making gifts of partial interest in a business is a very common business and estate planning technique.

Gifts often are not the entire answer, however. The amount that can be given away is limited. Everyone can gift up to $11,000 (indexed in the future to reflect inflation) to as many individuals as they wish each year. If the donor is married, and the spouse consents to the gift, that amount can be doubled. If more than that amount is gifted, a gift tax may be triggered. There is a lifetime gift tax exclusion, currently $1 million, which in the past was coordinated with the federal estate exclusion. The credit was called the "unified credit" reflecting the fact that the limit applied to the total of both lifetime gifts and transfers at death. The new law revised the federal estate tax rules, but did not change the rules for lifetime gifts. Each individual donor is entitled to utilize the maximum of $1 million during his or her lifetime for taxable gifts, but in years where the applicable credit is greater than $1 million, the balance is only available for transfers at death.

Although gifts are a valuable planning tool, they must be used with care so as not to upset the balance of the estate and business continuation planning.

### Charitable gifts

Another form of giving that often is used in estate and business planning is gifts to charity. These gifts can be made in any amount and are not impacted by the annual limit or the lifetime exclusion limit. The type of gift and the donor's income level limits the income tax deductibility of charitable gifts, however.

There are two aspects to the estate planning value of charitable gifts. The first is that charitable gifts reduce the amount of the taxable estate, thereby reducing the tax. The second is that there is an estate tax credit available to the estate owner for charitable bequests—which are essentially charitable gifts made at death. Charitable bequests are attractive because they save estate taxes due to a dollar-for-dollar reduction in the amount of the taxable estate, and they have the additional advantage of permitting the estate owner to enjoy the property during lifetime.

Charitable gifts and bequests are especially attractive to estate owners who have an interest in philanthropy. Together, the satisfaction of supporting worthy causes and the income and estate tax advantages of charitable giving makes these increasingly popular estate and business planning techniques.

## Conclusion

Again, estate planning is a very complex subject that can only be treated in-depth in one or more books. This chapter has been an attempt to hit the subject with a broad brush to give you a brief overview of some of the important issues to consider. The complexity of the subject means you must rely on your tax and financial advisors for advice pertaining to your situation. The laws, as we discussed, are in a state of almost constant change—which is another reason you will want to be sure you have adequate counseling before taking any action.

Benjamin Franklin said, "In this world nothing is certain but death and taxes." Keep that in mind as you plan for family wealth transfer. Remember above all that wealth transfer planning involving a family business must be undertaken with special care. Estate planning and business transfer planning becomes one topic. Don't plan your estate and business transfer separately. They are two aspects of a single problem. Plan them together using a single stable of advisors. Good luck!

# Chapter 10 summary points:

**In this chapter we discussed the fundamentals of estate planning:**

◈  **What is an estate?**

◈  **Basics of the estate tax**

◈  **Estate tax issues**

◈  **Gifts and gift taxes**

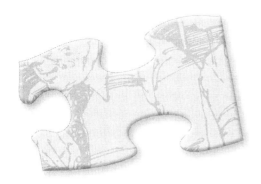

# Chapter 11

## Summary: Family & Business Renewal, a Proven Model

*Our real problem, then, is not our strength today; it is rather the vital necessity of action today to ensure our strength tomorrow.*

*—Dwight D. Eisenhower*

Well, we've come full circle. We started with a brief overview of the Model and worked our way through each of its three phases and nine steps. Let's step back and take another look at the big picture. Sometimes, in looking too closely at the details, we lose sight of the beginning, the middle and the end of a complex process. It's time to revisit the FBR diagram (which appears on the next page) and touch once again on the sequence and overall logic of the FBR System.

Recall that there are three legs representing the foundation of the FBR Model. The systematic process of family and business renewal embodied in the FBR System helps families and their businesses achieve these three goals: minimize the role of the IRS; enhance the quality of family life by promoting open, honest communication; and maximize business profitability by identifying appropriate and cost-effective wealth transfer solutions. All worthy objectives.

## Minimize IRS Role

One of the major goals of any business or wealth transfer plan is to minimize taxes and the role the IRS might otherwise play in the wealth transfer 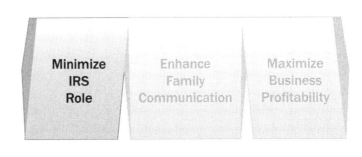 process. This is by and large the responsibility of a competent advisor. The training and experience of the Specialist can be helpful in weighing the various options available while planning. Knowledge of financial solutions, and legal and tax matters can all be very helpful.

One has to be careful when planning to minimize taxes, however.

Richard was a widower and his only son, Andy, had married his high school sweetheart, Jane. Andy and Jane had three beautiful children over the years. Richard, who had built a large cotton farm in Arizona, had a keen desire to ensure the IRS would get nothing when he died. His strategy was to make gifts of his business holdings to his son, Andy. Over the years, Richard gave Andy most all the business and many personal assets as well.

Unfortunately, Andy was killed in a hunting accident. Andy left all his assets to Jane, which initially caused no problems because of the great relationship Jane shared with her father-in-law, Richard. Later, Jane remarried. Unfortunately, Richard and her new husband, Adam, did not get along. In time, Adam managed to run Richard off the farm and even destroyed Richard's relationship with his grandchildren. Within a couple of years, Richard died brokenhearted and practically destitute. All this from a desire to eliminate taxation at death!

Planning for taxes and IRS involvement also requires consideration of the risk tolerance of the business owner and family members. An aggressive tax strategy might be comfortable for some, but far too risky for others.

Like everything else associated with the Model, the proper level of risk-taking in tax matters must be resolved, as much as possible, to everyone's satisfaction. In any case, the ultimate decision for specific tax strategies must be left in the hands of the family members and their advisors. The Specialist is wise to maintain a helpful stance, but not work to influence the decisions based on his or her own tolerance for risk-taking.

## Enhance Family Communication

Enhancing family communication is one of the core benefits of the Model. Virtually all wealth transfer succession planning includes analysis of ex-

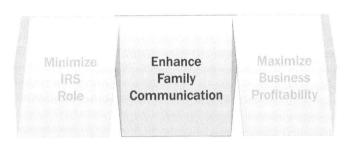

isting plans and study of alternatives for creating a new plan. The Model is unique in that it also seeks to improve the day-to-day communication among family members by treating the entire family as the client.

This may seem to some to be outside the scope of offering family business advice, but I maintain that this single feature impacts the ultimate success of the plan more than virtually anything else a planning advisor might do. Enhancing family communication does not appear as a phase or step in the Model, but rather is the result of the Model in action.

The enhancement begins with the individual family member interviews. In many cases, this part of the Model represents the first time an advisor has ever asked the opinion of family members regarding the business. The method used and the confidentiality of the process helps foster open and honest communication about the family and the business—again, probably for the first time.

The family retreat is a carefully structured opportunity for the family to communicate openly and honestly about the future of the business and each individual's expectation and concerns. An impartial third party acts as facilitator, mediator and wealth transfer planner. The net effect of all this, in many cases for the first time, is to open dialog about matters critical to the well being of both family and business.

Enriching the family's day-to-day interactions with each other is a powerful reason to use the Model. Anyone can crunch the numbers and develop a business wealth transfer plan, but it takes a special effort by someone like a trained Wealth Transfer Specialist to enhance family life in the process.

Here is an excerpt from a letter I received from a client addressing this very point.

> *We want you to know how appreciative we are of the work that you have done for our several family businesses. When you started wading through all of the issues and dealing with all of the family members, we could not have imagined that we would be able to resolve some of the difficulties that existed. This would not have been possible if you had not taken the personal interest in our businesses and in our family that you did. You really do offer a very valuable and unique service in that you have the financial expertise and the understanding of family dynamics.*
>
> *—S.K.*

Here's another example.

> *In today's world I am sure there are many families such as ours, who have special needs due to a second marriage with both the husband and wife having children from a first marriage.*
>
> *I know our family was a challenge, so many complex personalities and such strong-willed individuals. You handled the situation with such grace. We give you a great deal of credit.*
>
> *—R.E.*

## Maximize Business Profitability

Another underlying principle of the Model is to maximize the profitability of the business. Long-term planning for business transfer is a key part

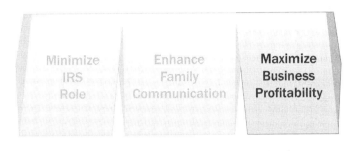

of this strategy. Without a plan for leadership succession, the future of the business remains under a cloud. This uncertainty affects not only family member security, but it also impacts employees—especially key employees—and even customers.

The best solution is for the business to create a well thought out plan for business succession and family wealth transfer. Once the plan is in place, it can be communicated to other individuals who have a need to know. The existence of a business succession plan can offer much reassurance to employees and others.

One successful dairyman I know has two boys in the business, but neither had ever been able to make management decisions because the father always wanted to control all the day-to-day operations. After I interviewed all the family members and facilitated a family meeting, everyone came to the conclusion that delegation of various duties and responsibilities was important and had to happen soon. The family decided to look at how they might improve their business operation and determine when, what and how the various operations should be conducted.

As a result of this planning, the boys have taken over the day-to-day operation of the business without their father's constant overview. This solution helps the business operate smoothly and permits the father to invest more of his time in long-range planning, other business interests and travel. In the past, due to confusion about roles and responsibilities, family members were never sure when they could take time off away from the business. As a result of the planning, family members can now easily determine time off and can mark it on the business calendar. This simple step has increased the quality of everyone's personal life by establishing a sense of balance between family and business.

The sons also agreed to buy out the parent's interest in the dairy so the other non-business family members could eventually receive their inheritance in the form of cash and notes receivable.

The results of these changes are that the family relationships have improved dramatically and business profits have increased. The quality of everyone's family life is enhanced. The parents are now pursuing activities that interest them and the business is thriving.

In addition to the benefits of security for family members and employees, working through the Model also can increase profitability by identifying real needs in the business and addressing them with appropriate, cost-effective solutions. For example, a buy-sell agreement may be determined to be the best alternative in a particular situation, but what is the best, most cost-effective means to fund the arrangement? The Specialist working with the FBR Model is in the best position to recommend solutions that make the most sense.

The Family & Business Renewal Model has three phases and nine steps. Let's briefly review the function and operation of each.

## Phase I: Understanding Objectives and the Current Plan

In Phase I we seek to understand the objectives of the family members as they relate to the business and understand the existing wealth transfer plan. If no plan currently exists, it means the family has delegated its long-term wealth planning to the state government via its laws of intestacy.

### Step 1: Interview individual family members.

The goal is to learn what each family member's hopes, dreams and expectations are with regard to the business. Understanding family dynamics is another goal of this step. FBR software automates and organizes this effort.

# The FBR Model
## 3 Phases, 9 Steps and 3 Benefits

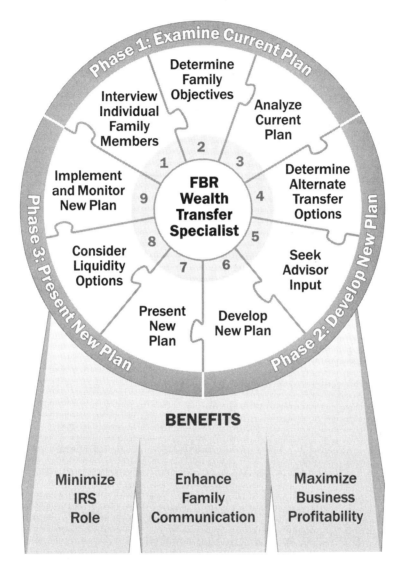

**BENEFITS**

Minimize IRS Role

Enhance Family Communication

Maximize Business Profitability

### Step 2: Identify family objectives.

This is a matter of taking the information gleaned from the individual interviews and boiling them down to the essential components. Reflecting on all the facts and feelings uncovered during the interviews; what are the basic goals of the family related to the business and its future?

### Step 3: Analyze the current plan.

This step requires examining the owner's existing personal and business documents related to the business or transfer of family wealth and capturing in some detail the terms of the current plan. The Specialist must be able to answer the question, "If the current owner dies, becomes disabled or retires tomorrow, what would happen to this business?"

## Phase II: Develop new plan

Phase II culminates in the design of a new wealth transfer plan.

### Step 4: Determine alternative wealth transfer options.

There are a number of ways wealth and property ownership can be transferred. The goal of this step is to study alternatives with the aim of identifying viable options that will work for this particular family.

### Step 5: Seek input from owner advisors.

In this step the Specialist convenes a meeting with each of the owner's trusted advisors. The goal is to obtain their input regarding the design of a new plan. Advisors also can provide a history of the existing plan and identify family concerns that could impact the design of the new plan.

### Step 6: Compile the new wealth transfer plan.

Taking into account everything that has been learned, the Specialist develops a new plan designed to meet as many individual family member goals as possible. The use of the FBR software expedites this practice.

## Phase III: Implement and track the new plan

Phase three is the final phase and the culmination of all the work that went before it.

### Step 7: The family retreat

The family is assembled in a neutral setting where the Specialist establishes a dialog regarding expectations, what is working and what changes need to be made. The Specialist explains both the current and the new plan and responds to questions and comments. The goal is to obtain agreement from the individual family members that this new plan is the best solution and should be implemented.

### Step 8: Consider the liquidity options.

Because one of the major problems facing most family business long-term planning is estate and business liquidity, the various options for providing it are examined in this step. The final choice is the one that best addresses the family and business needs.

### Step 9: Implement and monitor the new plan.

In this final step, the plan is actually implemented (legal documents executed, business agreements drafted and financial products sought, etc.) and a plan developed to monitor its progress continuously. The goal of this step is to make certain the entire plan is implemented and then kept up to date.

## The 12 Principles of Family & Business Renewal

We close our discussion of the FBR Model by briefly examining the twelve principles of family and business renewal.

### 1. It's a family affair—not just an owner's affair

One of the most unique aspects of the model is that it treats the entire family as the client, not just the business owner. This fact, by itself, assures a higher likelihood of success than a plan based simply on the owner's wishes without regard for the needs and concerns of other family members.

### 2. It's a process—not a transaction

A journey, not a destination is another way to think of the process. It is continuous and does not arrive at a solution cast in concrete for all time. Rather, the focus is on establishing effective family communication, examining all the information available, creating a suitable wealth transfer plan and then monitoring the new plan to keep it up to date.

### 3. It's an open agenda—not closed and secretive

One of the most common characteristics of the typical planning process is its focus on the wishes of the owner and his or her need to develop a plan in secret in order to avoid potential family conflict. The FBR Model is directly the opposite. No secrets. No hidden agendas. No problems later.

### 4. It's an asking format—not a telling one

The basis for the information gathering is the individual family member interviews. The Specialist asks questions about the needs, dreams and concerns of each family member and then considers that information when developing the new wealth transfer plan. Contrast that with the typical plan developed in secret and then announced to the family (possibly via the reading of the will/trust post-mortem). In many cases, the damaged family member relationships that result (e.g., siblings no longer speaking to each other) are frequently never fully mended.

### 5. It enhances the quality of family life through inclusion—not exclusion

Enhancing the quality of family communication is one of the foundational pillars of our Model. The key to it is inclusion. Individuals within the family are not left to worry and wonder about the wealth transfer plan and their role in it—they are included in the development of the plan from the start. The result is enhanced family trust.

### 6. It's a way to open family dialog and communication—not close discussion

Something important happens to families who learn to communicate through this procedure. They extend the newfound communication skills to other facets of family life. Once the family experiences open communication, it becomes a habit—just as failing to communicate once was.

### 7. It recognizes that the greatest resource is people—not plant, equipment and real estate

Andrew Carnegie once said, "Take away all my planes, trains, plants and equipment, but leave me my people and in two years I will have them all again." This model recognizes the most valuable asset any business has is its people. Take care of the people in the family business and most of the problems will take care of themselves.

### 8. It deals with both "external" and "internal" matters— not one at the expense of the other

Family issues that are "outside" of the business frequently have an impact on the day-to-day operation of the business, as well as its profitability. The Model recognizes this fact and includes matters typically thought of as outside the business, and therefore, not subject to scrutiny during the planning. All family matters—those internal or external to the operation of the business with the potential to impact its future—are included in the Renewal Process.

### 9. It ensures an examination of all issues—not a whitewash

Again, the open communication feature that is the hallmark of the process assures all issues of importance to the family and/or the business are considered. No legitimate concerns are glossed over or hidden under a cloak of secrecy.

### 10. It seeks input from owner advisors— not excluding any who might differ

The business advisor often is tempted to consider the advice of other advisors to the family—if they agree with them! The Model, being an open and honest approach to planning, encourages differences of opinions from advisors and others as part of the process of examining all aspects of the business and family needs and arriving at optimum solutions. This is a positive result of the value-added planning fee. Without it, the advisor often feels pressured to close transaction sales in order to be compensated.

### 11. It uses an objective Specialist who is a trained facilitator to conduct a family retreat—not a free-for-all anger tirade

Using the family retreat approach has many advantages, but it is possible that, poorly managed, it can deteriorate into an open family feud.

The facilitation skills of the Specialist is the best assurance that the family retreat will remain focused on the planning needs and end up as a positive experience for everyone.

### 12. It assures a money-back guarantee if not totally satisfied— not a risky venture

This feature protects both the business family and the Specialist. If the work is not satisfactory, the business receives a full refund of the fees paid. The presence of the money-back guarantee inhibits the Specialist from taking questionable cases just for the fee. If the client's circumstances are not a fit for the Model, the Specialist is unlikely to take the case because of the likely prospect of having to refund fees. Instead, the Specialist concentrates on viable family businesses where he or she can add value.

These twelve principles taken together outline the overwhelming advantage of the FBR Model to both the family, business and Specialist. Thorough, ethical, effective, satisfying—that is the Family & Business Renewal Model.

One of the best testimonials to the success of our Model that I've ever seen is the following letter from two business-owner parents to their daughter.

*Dear Alice,*

*The enclosed legal documents are evidence of our desire to share with you all of the blessings which may result from the ownership of the ranch.*

*In 1858 your great-grandparents left their mining operations and moved to this beautiful valley and acquired property bit by bit.*

*This property came to your father as a gift from his mother unencumbered.*

*The highest and best use of this land has been cattle rising, but for generations its greatest value has been the healthy, wholesome, character-building way of life for young people. We hope it can be preserved intact for the future generations of our family to enjoy in that way.*

*Our two daughters and our seven grandchildren have shared with us in the work and the pleasure of operating this cattle outfit. After 56 years of working together, we have this acreage free of debt. It gives us great pleasure to share the ownership with all of you.*

*The greatest value to us is our fine family, not only those of our issue, but our two sons-in-law, grandchildren and three great-grandchildren.*

*If this gift is received and held in the same sentiment and love in which it is given-for its moral and spiritual value, you will reap great benefits; but if it is treasured for its material value alone, the true riches will be lost sight of and strife could divide our blessed family.*

*Bear in mind what Jesus admonished his followers "seek ye first the king-dom of God and his righteousness and these things will be added onto you" Luke 12: 31.*

*With our love and faith in you,*

*Mom & Dad*

# Chapter 11 summary points:

**In this chapter we discussed:**

◈ **The benefits of the FBR Model**

   **Minimize the role of the IRS in the family business**

   **Maximize profitability of the business**

   **Enhance family communication**

◈ **Review of the three phases and nine steps of the FBR Model**

◈ **The twelve principles of the Family & Business Renewal Model**

# Epilogue

*Wealth comes in many forms and is not limited to green-backs or the numbers in a bank account. Health is wealth. The love and support of friends and family is wealth. Knowledge is wealth. The service that others offer, the products we use—all are forms of wealth. Defining our wealth on the basis of bank account numbers alone creates an artificial experience of poverty. It is artificial because every day one lives and is supported by the universe. This is cause for thanksgiving.*

*—John G. Boldt*

After much consideration, I have decided to share some thoughts about a personal philosophy that is an important part of both my business and my personal life. I believe that the quality of my life has been enhanced over the years by what I have learned from so many of my teachers, clients, friends and family, competitors and associates. My hope is that sharing these insights will assist you in your own personal search for inner peace.

For those who are not interested in continuing to read, I thank you for allowing me the opportunity to share my work experiences. I trust you will consider moving beyond the secretive, traditional planning to a more open wealth transfer process that concerns itself with both business profitability and quality of family life.

The subject of this book is the transfer of wealth, but as described in the quote above, wealth can be many things other than money and possessions. We should be thankful for all the forms of wealth we have been blessed with, but frequently, it is only after we have lost something that we truly recognize its value. We need to be thankful for each day we live and are supported by the universe.

The following thoughts are from lessons I've learned over the years that have enhanced the quality of my life. They fall into two broad categories or themes—the pursuit of material possessions and the search for inner peace. I would like to share some of the wealth from these experiences with you.

## Passion for Material Acquisition

We are all engaged in the pursuit of material acquisitions to some degree. The question is when does the pursuit become a passion and what does a passion for acquiring material possessions do to our concurrent search for inner peace?

### Who are we?

Are we human beings that happen to have a spirit or spiritual beings that happen to have a body? In order to have a sense of peace we need to know who we are. Over the years, I have invested much time and energy in keeping up my body, but as I grow older, I find myself more concerned about my spirit. Ask yourself, "Where am I investing my time and energy?" "Am I detaching myself from materialism in order to find more peace of mind or am I latching on to materialism in an effort to be more successful?" Real peace of mind comes from within—not through the accumulation of possessions.

### More versus better

I was talking with a very successful retired executive who told me his work goal had been to become a regional marketing vice president for a large national financial services company. After 30 years he achieved his work goal only to find out that it was not what he really wanted, after all.

He had paid a high price in terms of giving little or no attention to other aspects of his life. His experience taught me that I had better be sure that my goal is what I truly want because my family and I may be required to pay a great price for success.

Passion for the acquisition of material goods usually complicates our life rather than simplifies it. For many years a houseboat we owned on Lake Powell had been a source of much pleasure. However, as time went by, we found we were spending less and less time on the lake. One day, when I was examining our financial balance sheet, I noted the boat was listed as an asset. The truth of the matter was we were still paying for the upkeep of the boat and many other related expenses, but we were no longer using it. The houseboat was actually more a liability than an asset at that point. We finally decided to sell the boat.

Establishing greater simplicity in our lives is often overlooked in favor of obtaining more material goods. But accumulating assets usually results in additional complexity. We sometimes live by the motto that more is better, but we frequently work harder to buy more things only to find out that we paid too high a price. As Ralph Waldo Emerson once said, "Money costs too much."

### Living in the present

I recall that much of my life had been spent in regrets about the past or anxiety about the future. The ego seems to have a vested interest only in the past or future. Staying in the present moment is a luxury that many of us are unable to obtain. However, spending time on guilt or regret about past failings is living in the past. Worry or anxiety is attempting to live in the future. The past is gone. The future is promised to no one. Resolve to live in the present—it's all we really have. Life lived to the highest level of selflessness is the ideal.

### Relativity

We often tend to want to label experiences as good or bad. For many years I thought I knew the difference between good and bad and made judgments accordingly. However, sometimes I found that an experience

I had labeled bad turned out to be good and vice-versa. The following personal story is an example of what I mean.

I conducted my business traveling in six Western states. Most of my planning work was done in rural communities that were not served by public transportation. As a result, I frequently drove for long distances and, in some cases, even that was not a practical solution because of the distances involved. In an effort to cut down my travel time, I bought an airplane and hired a pilot. This was good because it cut my travel time dramatically and increased my ability to serve more clients. However, it increased the cost of my travel, which was bad. Later, in order to travel at night and during poor weather conditions, I acquired a twin engine plane. That was good—except it required a substantial capital investment and dramatically increased operating costs, which was bad. After several years had gone by, I attempted to reduce my business operating costs by decreasing the amount of insurance I carried on the aircraft. That was good because the premiums were less, but shortly thereafter, I had an aircraft accident, and the insurance company paid less than the full cost of the damage—which was bad. The lesson I learned from this experience is that some situations are not necessarily what they first appear to be.

### Maintaining balance in our lives

Most of us recognize the importance of maintaining balance in our lives. However, paying lip service to the concept is quite different from actually putting it into practice. We are all pulled in many directions at once by virtue of being a spiritual person, spouse, parent, community volunteer, employee, etc. The realization that I should devote more time, energy and activity to my family came much more easily than actually giving my wife and family more quality time. Then I discovered that by expanding my personal identity to include my family, I could begin to make progress. I began to feel that my success extended beyond financial success to include success in participating in family life. I became more aware of their needs, interests and moods. Giving them time and energy became less of a sacrifice and more of a genuine desire. As I shared their interests they became more open to my interests; our family seemed to draw together into a more cohesive unit, a team.

Attempting to maintain balance often feels like trying to keep several basketballs bouncing at the same time. Each ball requires the same attention. If we concentrate on any one of them, the others begin to loose their energy. It is very difficult, but not impossible, to keep them all bouncing with the same intensity. Life isn't exactly like that, however. It's impossible to pay equal attention, at all times, to every aspect of one's life. Some parts require more attention at times than others. Better to think of the various aspects of life as parts of a single ball. Concentrate on living the one life you have to the fullest. Don't waste life trying for perfection in every aspect of it. Bouncing one ball is much easier.

Recently Donna, a client of mine, shared the following sentiment:

*Words to Live By*

*A master of the art of living draws no sharp distinction between work and play. His labor and leisure, his mind and body, his education and recreation—he hardly knows which is which. He simply pursues his vision of excellence through whatever he is doing and leaves others to determine whether he is working or playing; to him he always seems to be doing both.*

*—Author Unknown*

## The Quest for Inner Peace

The pursuit of material possessions does not lead to inner peace. The quest for inner peace is a separate mission that requires a certain detachment from materialism. The focus is internal rather than external.

### Finding peace of mind

Much of my life has been devoted to keeping my mind busy. For a long time I had little or no time for reflection because my ego always seemed to have so much to contribute. It was a blessing for me to learn how to still my mind so I could focus on a higher sense of awareness. The key for me has been to adopt a regimen of practicing silent meditation daily. I found that as I focused less on material success and more on my family, I became more aware of my spirit. And, as I became more aware of my spirit and what nourished it, my mind grew less agitated. Instead of needing distraction, I was rested and strengthened by quieting the mind. Into the quiet of my mind came thoughts and feelings about God.

Previously, my mind could not be at peace because of the constant urge to always be more active rather than less. Now, with my mind at peace, my heart also seems to be more engaged. Stilling the mind and engaging the heart eliminates the need for constant judgment and encourages greater acceptance of oneself and others. As a result, my life is now focused on cooperation rather than competition.

Years ago while in Portland visiting a teacher, I was eating breakfast and reading a book he had written. He came into the room, took the book from me and threw it on the floor. As I picked up the book, I asked him why he had thrown it to the floor. He responded that it was important to always focus on one matter at a time. He believed reading while eating demonstrates lack of focus—the result being that neither is done well. Part of stilling the mind is developing the ability to focus with an open mind and heart.

I like the way the classic Sanskrit chant addresses peace:

*Lead us from the unreal to the real.*

*Lead us from darkness to light.*

*Lead us from death to immortal life.*

*Peace, peace, peace.*

### Understanding other's beliefs

During a motor home trip through an Indian reservation, my wife Lillian and I stopped along the road to attend a tent revival meeting. We were the only non-Native Americans attending and were warmly greeted. Shortly after being seated, a grandmother came up to us with a smile, and without a word, presented Lillian with an infant to hold. The baby lay contentedly in Lillian's arms through the entire service. Later, we asked others why this woman shared this infant with us and were told that this was her way of thanking us for attending. What a gift she gave us!

During the meeting the lay minister informed us that in his previous faith he was able to see God in the streams, trees, valleys, skies and mountains. He seemed somewhat saddened as he explained that now, with his new religion, he needed to wait until his death to see God. I wondered about the person who had convinced this Native American to replace his former belief with another.

As a youngster growing up, I once asked a neighbor how it was possible that God would save only those who shared our particular beliefs, when the majority of the world's population believes differently. I don't recall his response, but many years later the question was finally put to rest for me when I learned teachings that maintain all paths lead to God. What a relief it was to know that I did not have to attempt to save lost souls who believed differently.

### Process versus results

In our culture, with its focus on results, it would appear that results are key and how they are achieved doesn't usually matter—"I don't care how you do it, just get it done!" Yet the satisfaction of achieving results is often short-lived because we are always immediately dashing off, pursuing our next goal. Enron, WorldCom, and Global Crossings are corporate examples of the same phenomenon.

Most of my early years were devoted to getting desired results. At times I even prayed that God would assist me in achieving my materialistic goals. Results meant everything to me. Then I met a man who I believed to be a great teacher. I told him of my interest in becoming his student. He asked me many questions, including what I expected to learn and how long I planned to be a student. To my great surprise he rejected me as a student. He explained that my expectations were unrealistic in view of my impatience. He suggested another teacher who he believed could meet my needs within the short time period I had established.

In retrospect, I realized this man was a great teacher! He was more interested in helping me meet my expectations than he was in increasing the number of students. I decided this was the kind of person I wanted to become.

Over the years my need to focus on results has waned. Now my attention is more on the journey and less on the destination. This has allowed me to maximize my focus on the process and minimize my obsession with the outcome. The benefit is a greater sense of selfless service and less anxiety about getting selfish results.

## The Butterfly

I'd like to leave you with this story. Think of it when you find life's experiences difficult to deal with.

*A man found a cocoon. One day a small opening appeared, he sat and watched the butterfly for several hours as it struggled to force its body through the little hole. Then it seemed to stop making any progress. It appeared as if it had gotten as far as it could and could go no farther. Then the man decided to help the butterfly. He took a pair of scissors and snipped the remaining bit of the cocoon. The butterfly then emerged easily. Something was strange. The butterfly had a swollen body and shriveled wings. The man continued to watch the butterfly because he expected at any moment, the wings would enlarge and expand to be able to support the body, which would contract in time.*

*Neither happened. In fact, the butterfly spent the rest of its life crawling around with a swollen body and deformed wings. It was never able to fly.*

*What the man in his kindness and haste did not understand, was that the restricting cocoon and the struggle required for the butterfly to get through the small opening of the cocoon are God's way of forcing fluid from the body of the butterfly into its wings so that it would be ready for flight once it achieved its freedom from the cocoon.*

*Sometimes struggles are exactly what we need in our life. If God allowed us to go through all our life without any obstacles, that would cripple us. We would not be as strong as what we could have been. Not only that, we could never fly.*

*—Origin Unknown*

We need to struggle to grow from life's challenges so that, unlike the butterfly in the story, we are able to meet all that life offers. As a great teacher once said, "Go beyond both fear of pain and search for pleasure."

# Glossary of Terms

## Buy-Sell (or Business Continuation) Agreement

A buy-sell agreement, sometimes called a business continuation agreement, is a legally binding agreement to sell your business for a stated price upon your death, disability or other lifetime sale. The agreed-on price, or pricing formula, may fix the value of the business interests for estate tax purposes. However, there must be a business purpose for the agreement, and the value of the business interest must be determined through an "arm's length" valuation process.

There are two basic types of buy-sell agreements: stock redemption (or entity agreement) where the business purchases a decedent's business interest; and cross-purchase where the business interest is purchased by surviving partners or co-stockholders of the deceased owner.

## Business Life Insurance

Business life insurance usually insures the life of a person involved in a business either as an owner or key employee. Generally, the business owns the insurance, pays the premiums and is beneficiary. The proceeds of business life insurance are intended to be used for business purposes.

## Business Organizations

### Corporation

A legal entity created under state statutes that generally has the same rights and powers to carry on business as an individual. A corporation can own property and sue or be sued. Corporations are owned by their shareholders and operated by corporate officers appointed directly or indirectly by them. Shareholders have limited liability, meaning they generally are not personally liable for the debts of the corporation.

Ownership of a corporation is represented by one or more classes of stock, owned by shareholders, which can be transferred freely. A corporation can be classified a "C Corporation" or "S Corporation."

A "C Corporation" is subject to income taxes on its profits. Income from profits paid to owners, in the form of corporate dividends, is also subject to ordinary income taxation at the individual's personal tax rate. This so-called "double taxation" is one disadvantage of the corporate form of business organization.

An "S Corporation" is a corporation that has elected special tax treatment. This tax treatment allows an "S Corporation" to pass income directly through to the corporate owners without a corporate income tax. The income is taxed as personal income to the individuals. The result is that "S Corporation" income is taxed only once. In addition, losses of the corporation generally pass through to the shareholders and can then be used by them to offset other income.

### General Partnership

An association in which all members carry on a trade or business for the joint benefits and profit of the owners or partners. A partnership will generally terminate at the death of any of the partners, unless the partnership agreement itself or some other agreement provides for the continuation of the partnership business after the death of a partner.

Each partner normally has an equal voice in the management of the business and shares to some degree in partnership income and losses. Unlike a "C Corporation," there is no separate partnership income tax. Partners are taxed on profits at their personal tax rate.

Each partner has unlimited liability for partnership debts and liabilities. In addition, the transfer of a partnership interest is generally subject to the approval of the remaining partners.

### Limited Liability Company (LLC)

The limited liability company (LLC) is a business organization which is used to obtain the advantages of limited liability for owners (called "members"). As with the corporate structure, LLC members are not liable for debts beyond their investment in the business. An LLC can choose to be taxed as a partnership meaning it is not subject to a separate corporate tax. Additionally, any losses incurred by the LLC will be passed through and be deductible by the members under the partnership rules.

From the estate planning standpoint, a major advantage of an LLC classified as a partnership is that, upon the death of a member, the LLC may elect to adjust the basis of its assets to fair market value to the extent of the decedent's interest.

### Limited Partnership

In a limited partnership, there are one or more general partners who manage the business and who share in the income and losses of the partnership. In addition, there must be one or more limited partners who share in some form in the partnership income, but whose liability is limited to the extent of their investment in the partnership.

The transfer of a limited partnership interest may be subject to the approval of the remaining general and/or limited partners. To overcome this limitation, the partnership agreement is sometimes written in such a way as to provide for the transfer of a limited partnership interest without the approval of the remaining partners.

### Sole Proprietorship

A business owned and generally managed by a single individual. The owner has full control of the business and unlimited responsibility for any losses or liabilities. Business terminates at death.

### Charitable Gift

A charitable gift is a transfer of a present interest (or a future remainder interest) in property to a public entity or to a corporation or organization for religious, scientific, literary or educational uses. The value of property qualifying as a charitable gift may qualify for a full or partial income tax deduction and also be deducted in its entirety from the gross estate.

## Corporate Reorganization

Family owned corporations are sometimes reorganized as a means of restructuring for tax or other reasons. One type of corporate reorganization is a recapitalization of a corporation to provide for two classes of stock. The owner of one class, called preferred stock, usually has the right to a fixed annual dividend, the right to receive assets of the corporation ahead of other stockholders upon dissolution and the right to vote for the board of directors. Preferred stock may also have cumulative or non-cumulative dividend features.

The other class, called common stock, will appreciate and depreciate in value as economic conditions and the fortunes of the business fluctuate. Common stockholders generally control the business through their ability to vote for the board of directors, but in the case of the family reorganization, the common stock is usually non-voting. Typically, the current owners keep the preferred stock and gift the shares of common stock to the future owners.

### Discounted Dollars

The "discounted dollars" concept refers to funds received as life insurance proceeds which are purchased by means of yearly premiums. They are called discounted dollars because each dollar of death proceeds is purchased for a fraction of the amount eventually to be received. The size of the fraction depends on the type of policy purchased, how long the insured lives and on whether he/she qualified for preferred, standard or substandard rates.

### Economic Growth & Tax Relief Reconciliation Act of 2001 (EGTRRA)

The Economic Growth and Tax Relief Reconciliation Act of 2001 (EGTRRA) gradually reduces the maximum estate tax rate and phases in a number of incremental increases to the estate tax credit. These changes are reflected in the chart on the next page. The "applicable exclusion amount" is the dollar amount the unified credit allows to pass estate tax-free. As you can see, the amount of property passing tax-free increases in a series of steps from 2002 through 2010, when the estate tax is fully repealed. However, all of the changes made by this law will "sunset" after December 31, 2010. Thus, as of January 1, 2011, the tax law reverts to what it was before this legislation was enacted. As a result, the estate tax goes back into effect, and the applicable exclusion amount reverts to $1 million, just as it was before EGTRRA became law.

| Year | Top Estate Tax Rate | Applicable Exclusion Amount |
|------|---------------------|-----------------------------|
| 2002 | 50% | $1,000,000 |
| 2003 | 49% | $1,000,000 |
| 2004 | 48% | $1,500,000 |
| 2005 | 47% | $1,500,000 |
| 2006 | 46% | $2,000,000 |
| 2007 | 45% | $2,000,000 |
| 2008 | 45% | $2,000,000 |
| 2009 | 45% | $3,500,000 |
| 2010 | Zero tax; estate tax repealed for one year | |
| 2011 | 50% | $1,000,000 |

## Estate Shrinkage

Last illness and funeral expenses, administrative costs and death taxes.

## Gifts

A gift is a complete transfer of ownership rights in property from one individual to another or to an entity such as a trust. Each individual has the ability to gift property up to the amount of the annual exclusion ($11,000 in 2002, indexed for inflation) to an unlimited number of donees. A married couple, with both spouses consenting to the gift, may give up to $22,000 each year to any number of individuals. Gifts in excess of the annual exclusion amount become subject to the applicable exclusion amount (currently $1 million).

Once the total of gifts in excess of the annual exclusion exceeds the applicable exclusion amount, the excess is subject to gift taxes. The calculation of the tax is the same as the calculation for estate taxes with one difference: while EGTRRA gradually increases the amount exempted from estate taxation up to 2011, the gift tax exclusion equivalent remains at $1 million. (See *Economic Growth & Tax Relief Reconciliation Act of 2001*.)

## Heirs

### Business Heir

Heir or heirs who will succeed to the actual ownership and operation of the business.

### Non-business Heir

Heir or heirs not actively involved in the operation of the business.

## Marital Deduction

In estate taxation, the amount of property a deceased person can give outright or in a special trust to the surviving spouse without estate taxation. Unlimited since 1982.

## Power of Attorney (Durable)

A durable power of attorney is a legal document that enables the creator to appoint one or more persons to act on his/her behalf in business or personal matters, even if he/she becomes incapacitated or disabled.

## Private Annuity

Private annuity as used herein is an unsecured promise by the transferee(s) of property to make periodic payments in a specified amount to the transferor(s) during their joint or separate lives or for a specified period of time.

## Property Ownership

### *Community Property*

A form of property ownership that exists only between husband and wife who are considered to have an undivided one-half interest in such property during marriage. An asset acquired with funds earned during a marriage while a resident of a community property state is, by nature, community property. Assets acquired in the name of either spouse are presumed to be community property. The decedent's interest in community property may be controlled by his/her will.

### *Joint Tenancy and Tenancy by the Entirety*

Joint tenancy and tenancy by the entirety are forms of joint property ownership by two or more persons with right of survivorship. When a joint tenant dies, his or her interest in the property automatically goes to the surviving joint tenant outside of and beyond the power of the will of the deceased joint tenant; the property also passes outside of probate. Tenancy by the entirety can only be created by a husband and wife.

### *Tenancy in Common*

Tenancy in common is another form of joint ownership of property whereby each tenant has a fractional, divisible interest in the property. Two or more persons as tenants in common may hold title to real or personal property. Because there is no right of survivorship, the legal relationships and results are very different from joint tenancy. A major difference is that each tenant has the right to leave his or her share of the property to someone other than a co-tenant at death.

### *Life Estate*

A life estate is an interest in property, the term of which is measured by the life of its owner or some other person.

## Sinking Fund

A fund designed to accumulate over a period of years, by means of regular deposits and earned interest. A sinking fund is usually used to meet a future cash outlay that is expected to occur at a specified time.

## Stepped-up Basis

The tax basis of some types of property acquired from a decedent is stepped-up (or stepped-down) to fair market value at the date of death. Thus, if the heir sells the property, no income or capital gains tax is paid on the appreciation occurring before date of death. If the property value is stepped down at death, no loss attributable to a decline in value occurring before the date of death can be deducted for income tax purposes.

## Stock Redemption (Section 303)

Section 303 of the Internal Revenue Code establishes a way for a corporation to make a distribution in redemption of a portion of a decedent's stock that will not be taxed as a dividend. A Section 303 partial redemption can provide cash and/or other property from the corporation to the decedent shareholder's estate for death taxes and other expenses.

## Trusts

A trust arises when a property owner transfers legal title of the property to an individual who controls and manages the property for the benefit of another, subject to the terms of a trust agreement. The beneficial interest in the trust property may belong to the trustee or to any other individual, so long as there is not a sole trustee and a sole beneficiary who is the same person. A trustee may be either a corporation, such as bank or trust company, or an individual.

### By-pass Provisions

By-pass provisions are used herein to designate that language in a trust or will necessary to avoid property being taxed in the estate of the second spouse to die. These provisions are inserted in either a living trust or a testamentary trust and often are used synonymously with "family trust."

## *Charitable Remainder Trust*

This device enables an individual to make a deferred gift to a charity while retaining the right to payments of income from the trust. Terms of the trust can provide that income from its invested assets is paid to the grantor, but when the grantor dies, the remaining value in the trust is distributed to the charitable beneficiaries. Contributing an asset to this trust provides an income tax deduction. The amount of the deduction varies based on the age or ages of the grantors, the value of the property donated and the design of the trust. Because the beneficiaries are charities, trust earnings are exempt from income and capital gains taxes. If land is donated to a charitable remainder trust and the land is sold by the trust, for example, no tax is due from the grantor or the trust. When the grantor dies, the assets in this trust will not be subject to death taxes.

## *Family Trust*

Also called an exemption trust or by-pass trust. May be established in a living trust or in a will. Upon death, the trust becomes irrevocable and is designed to benefit the surviving spouse while at the same time taking advantage of estate tax savings. The surviving spouse generally is given the right to receive the income from the trust assets for life and limited rights to receive principal for specified purposes. The surviving spouse can also be given a limited power to appoint a restricted number of persons who are to receive the assets at the surviving spouse's death.

The purpose of the trust is to insure the financial security of a surviving spouse without subjecting the assets in the trust to estate taxes at the death of the surviving spouse.

## *Generation-Skipping Trust*

A generation-skipping trust is defined as any trust that has beneficiaries that are more than one generation younger than the grantor (e.g., grandchildren, great-grandchildren, etc.). Only a trust that has beneficiaries in at least two generations, both of which are below the grantor's generation, is a generation-skipping trust.

### Wealth Replacement Trust

A trust that transfers any right to alter, amend, revoke or terminate the trust to an appointed trustee. A transfer of property to such a trust constitutes a gift. The trustee can purchase life insurance that will pass income and estate tax-free. Often used to compensate heirs for assets given away (to a charity, for example) by an estate owner.

### Living Trust (Revocable)

A trust in which the person setting up the trust retains the right to alter, amend, revoke and/or terminate the trust. When a living trust is used, the trust assets will be included in the taxable estate of the person setting up the trust. Living trusts are used to avoid probate and to facilitate the timely, private transfer of assets at death.

### Marital Trust

A trust established by a will or revocable living trust for the benefit of a surviving spouse that minimizes or eliminates estate taxes in the deceased spouse's estate. (See *Marital Deduction* & *Unlimited Marital Deduction*).

### QTIP Trust

A Qualified Terminable Interest Property (QTIP) trust is a means of utilizing the unlimited marital deduction for federal estate tax purposes. It may be used in conjunction with a family (credit shelter) trust. The QTIP trust is used when a married person wishes to retain ultimate disposition power over his/her property after death. All of the property placed in the QTIP trust is for the surviving spouse's benefit so long as he/she lives, but upon his/her death, the provisions of the trust dictate who will receive the remaining assets in the trust.

### Unlimited Marital Deduction

The unlimited marital deduction enacted into law in 1982 allows the deceased spouse to pass any or all of his/her property to a surviving spouse (who is a U.S. citizen), free of estate taxes. The gift tax exclusion between spouses is likewise unlimited.

# Resources

Allred, Roger C. & Allred, Russel S. *The Family Business: Power Tools for Survival, Success and Succession*. Berkley. 1997

Bareither, Karl R. *Planning a Family & Business Legacy: A Holistic Approach to Wealth Transfer Planning for Entrepreneurs, Business Owners & Family Members*. FBR. 2003

*The Big Kahuna*. Dir. John Swanbeck. Perf. Kevin Spacey, Danny DeVito, Peter Facinelli. Universal Studios. 2000

Bork, David. *Family Business, Risky Business*. Aspen, CO: Bork Institute for Family Business 1993

Bork, Davis et al. *Working with Family Businesses: A Guide for Professionals*. San Francisco: Jossey-Bass, Inc. 1996

Cahoon, David K. & Gibbs, Larry W. with Mike Nall. *Strictly Business: Strategies for Privately Owned Businesses*. Denver, CO. Quantum Press. 2002

Cohn, Mike. *Passing the Torch*. New York: McGaw-Hill, inc. 1992

*Country*. Dir Richard Pearce. Perf. Jessica Lang, Sam Shephard, Wilford Brimley. Touchstone Films. 1984

Danco. Katy. *From the Other Side of the Bed: A Woman Looks at Life in the Family Business*. Cleveland: The University Press, Inc. 1981

Dreuex, Dirk R. & Goodman, Joe M. *Business Succession Planning and Beyond: A Multi-disciplinary Approach to Representing the Family-Owned Business*. The American Bar Association. 1997

Family Firm Institute Web site, various articles, at *http://www.ffi.org*.

Goleman, Daniel. *Emotional Intelligence*. New York, NY: Bantam Books. 1995

Jaffe, Dennis T. *Working with the Ones You Love*. Emeryville, CA: Conari Press. 1991

Jones, H. Stanley. *Marketing Your Financial Planning Services: A Guide for Professionals*. New York: John Wiley & Sons, Inc. 1988

Kinder, George. *The Seven Stages of Money Maturity*. New York, NY: Delacorte Press. 1999

LeVan, Gerald. *Getting to Win-Win in Family Business*. Alexander, North Carolina: WorldComm Press. 1993

Wilson, Larry. *Changing the Game: The New Way to Sell*. New York, NY: Simon & Schuster. 1987

# FBR Fact Finder Forms

The following pages contain reproductions of some of the pages of the FBR System Fact Finder. All the pages are not reproduced here because of space limitations. In total, there are over fifty pages to the paper fact finder. Many pages are duplicates. For example, there are several identical pages available for the family interviews to provide sufficient space for interviewing numerous individuals.

In addition to the pages reproduced here, there are other pages used to gather information about the family and business finances, existing wills and trusts.

In addition to the personal and business information, the Fact Finder also includes pages that help you summarize the family's objectives—those achieved and not achieved.

The balance of the fact finder consists of pages of recommendations and conclusions. These are used to identify the recommendations and conclusions the Specialist wishes to include in the final report. The recommendations and conclusions contained in the Fact Finder match those found in the FBR software. By completing the paper Fact Finder pages, the Specialist can organize the information for easier entry into the FBR software.

The pages reproduced here will give you an idea of the type of information obtained about the family and the business, and the format of the Fact Finder itself.

# Wealth Transfer Specialist Information

**Date** _____

**Wealth Transfer Specialist** _____

**How originated?** _____

- When is this plan needed? _____

- Additional data forthcoming from client? _____

- Client contact for additional information _____

  _____

  _____

- Best time? _____

- Contact Advisors for input before plan is started? _____

  After? _____

- Any additional comments regarding client's plan?

  _____

  _____

  _____

  _____

# Family Fact Finder

|  | Owner | Co-Owner/Spouse |
|---|---|---|
| **Name** | | |
| Nickname | | |
| Birthdate | | |
| Birthplace | | |
| Home Address | | |
| Home Phone | | |
| Work Address | | |
| Work Phone | | |
| Occupation | | |
| Mother | | |
| Mother's DOB | | |
| Father | | |
| Father's DOB | | |
| Health | | |

Comments (problems, employment, etc.) _____

_____

_____

_____

_____

|  | Child | Spouse |
|---|---|---|
| **Name** | | |
| Nickname | | |
| Birthdate | | |
| Birthplace | | |
| Home Address | | |
| Home Phone | | |
| Occupation | | |

Comments (children, problems, health, employment, etc.) _____

_____

_____

_____

|  | Child | Spouse |
|---|---|---|
| **Name** | | |
| Nickname | | |
| Birthdate | | |
| Birthplace | | |
| Home Address | | |
| Home Phone | | |
| Occupation | | |

Comments (children, problems, health, employment, etc.) _____

_____

_____

_____

# Owner Advisors

| | Attorney | Accountant |
|---|---|---|
| **Name** | | |
| Address | | |
| Phone | | |
| Advised since | | |

Comments _____
_____
_____
_____
_____
_____

| | Insurance/Financial Advisor | Banker |
|---|---|---|
| **Name** | | |
| Address | | |
| Phone | | |
| Advised since | | |

Comments _____
_____
_____
_____
_____
_____

|  | **Other Trusted Advisor** | **Other Trusted Advisor** |
|---|---|---|
| **Name** | | |
| Address | | |
| Phone | | |
| Advised since | | |

Comments _____

_____

_____

_____

_____

# Family Business Facts

**Company Name** _____

Address _____

_____

## Ownership

☐  Sole Proprietor

☐  Partnership:       ☐  General Partnership       ☐  Limited Partnership

☐  Corporation:       ☐  C Corporation             ☐  S Corporation

Stock Shares:        _____ Common        _____ Preferred

| Name | Title | Ownership % | Value | Discounted Value? |
|---|---|---|---|---|
|  |  |  |  |  |
|  |  |  |  |  |
|  |  |  |  |  |
|  |  |  |  |  |

Nature of business _____

Date established _____     Last appraisal date _____

Key people _____

_____

Current business market value _____

Market value for determining ownership _____

Are there any written business agreements? _____

_____

_____

_____

# Family Interview Guide

**Family Member** _____

Describe your major concerns regarding the business.

_____

_____

_____

How do these affect you and other family members, now and in the future?

_____

_____

_____

In what areas does your family communicate effectively?

_____

_____

_____

In what areas does your family communicate poorly?

_____

_____

_____

Over what issues and between which individuals do you experience communication breakdown?

_____

_____

_____

_____

Are you in favor of the business continuing in this or another form?

_____

_____

_____

If not, what would you like to see happen?

_____

_____

_____

Do you think your family members work together productively?

_____

_____

_____

What are your suggestions for improving productivity?

_____

_____

_____

What additional information would be important for me to understand to assist your family or business?

_____

_____

_____

_____

_____

_____

# Business Continuation Overview

**In the event of death, should the business be sold or retained?**

_____

**If the business is to be retained:**

- Who in the family is qualified to assume control? _____

  _____

- If more than one person is qualified, to whom should control pass?

  _____

- If there is more than one heir, how should the estate to be distributed?

  _____

  _____

  _____

  _____

  _____

**If the business is to be sold:**

- Who would purchase the business? _____

  _____

- Are there any agreements regarding a sale now in effect? _____

  _____

  _____

- Is the agreed upon selling price currently correct? _____

- Is there a provision for valuation update? _____

# Planning Objectives

**Name** _____

**Personal**

☐ To maintain financial security during your lives

☐ To maintain flexibility during your lives

**Family**

☐ To minimize potential family conflicts

☐ To treat your heirs fairly upon your demise

☐ To treat your heirs equally upon your demise

☐ To achieve the above and maintain flexibility

**Business**

☐ To gradually turn over business operation to your business heirs

☐ To pass the business intact to your heirs

☐ To create a more business-like approach

**Financial**

☐ To minimize your estate taxes

☐ To minimize administration costs at death

☐ To facilitate gifts to your heirs

# Client Planning Fee Agreement
(SAMPLE)

_____, client, hereby subscribes to this Family Business Renewal Agreement. Client agrees to pay fees as stated. All FBR planning fees are based on a formula that takes into account the complexity, size of family, asset values, number of organizations and the scope of the work to be completed. *A money-back guarantee, if not totally satisfied, is your assurance of FBR's quality renewal service.*

## Phase I: Examining the Present Plan

Involves interviewing each individual family member and spouse, identifying family objectives, and analyzing the existing plan. Client agrees to provide any and all information required to accurately reflect current family, business and financial conditions. All information given will remain confidential. It will not be used for any purpose other than to develop the new plan. As facts and opinions are gathered, a complete portrait of the family, business and financial information will emerge.

$ _____

## Phase II: Developing the FBR Process

Includes examining alternative transfer methods, seeking input from your advisors, and writing new plan. Client authorizes the FBR Wealth Transfer Specialist (Specialist) to contact client advisors to obtain all necessary information for the preparation of the written new plan.

$ _____

## Phase III: Implementing the FBR Process

Includes presenting a written plan at a family retreat with all family members and spouses present. Candid discussions are facilitated by the FBR Specialist. Financial options are considered. The FBR Specialist, acting as facilitator, works with the client's trusted advisors to assure the implementation and tracking of the process in a timely manner.

$ _____

The FBR Specialist will not provide any tax or legal advice and will not prepare legal documents to implement any plan. Any implementation of the plan is the responsibility of the contracting client and his or her legal and tax advisors.

The parties recognize that financial plan projections are based on the information provided by client, assumptions of tax effects, and present economic conditions, all of which may fluctuate. Therefore, no warranties can be made that the client's goals will be reached. With regard to the services performed pursuant to the terms of this agreement, FBR Specialist will not be liable to client, or to anyone who may claim any right due to his or her relationship to the client, for any acts or omissions in the performance of said services except when said acts or omissions of the FBR Specialist are due to willful misconduct. Client shall hold the FBR Specialist free and harmless from any obligations or claims arising out of the FBR services.

**Client:**                                    **FBR Specialist:**


_____          _____
Signature                                      Signature


_____          _____
Name                                           Name


_____          _____
Date                                           Date

# Family Business and Estate Analysis and Wealth Transfer Plan for Jack and Genny Royce and Family

(SAMPLE)

Prepared by Karl R. Bareither,
Wealth Transfer Specialist

December 3, 1998

This sample FBR report provides some of the pages of a proposed new wealth transfer plan for a fictitious family and is for illustration purposes only. It does not necessarily reflect the typical size or complexity of actual cases encountered. Real life cases may consist of larger or smaller businesses and family net worth may be more or less than illustrated here. This sample also should not be viewed as an accurate presentation of current tax laws. An actual report would, of course, contain accurate information about the family and business and reflect all applicable tax laws in effect at the time the document is prepared.

FBR System, Inc. is not engaged in the practice of law and does not offer legal, tax, accounting or financial advice. The facts displayed within this report are fictitious. Any resemblance to actual persons living or deceased is strictly coincidental.

# Review of Current Estate Plan

## CURRENT WILL OF JACK & GENNY ROYCE

Date of Will: November 2, 1993; 1st Codicil & 2nd amend to trust 10/2/98

Executor: Surviving Spouse

Successor Executor: Phillip Royce, or Sarah Royce if he ceases to act

Distribution of Estate: By Will and Trust for Jack & Genny Royce

### At the death of the first spouse:

All personal property of a personal nature including but not limited to, furniture, appliances, automobiles, jewelry, artifacts, and other personal effects shall be bequeathed to spouse, provided they survive more than 60 days. If they do not then all of the above said property will be added to the residue of the estate.

The residue of the estate will be bequeathed, in trust to the Trustee of that trust designated as the Trust of Jack Royce and Genny Royce.

### At the death of the second spouse:

The Trustee may pay out of the principal of the Survivor's Trust or if it has been exhausted, out of the Marital Trust or the Exemption Trust the Survivor's debts, last illness and funeral expenses, fees and other costs incurred in administering the probate estate, termination of this trust estate and inheritance taxes.

A disinterested, qualified appraiser shall appraise the entire remaining tangible personal property. Each of the Settlor's living children (Sally Royce, Tom Royce, Phillip Royce, Wendy Royce & Robert Lansing) shall be entitled to an equal share of the said tangible property. The living children shall be given chits in the amount of $100.00 denomination totaling the amount of their respective share. Thereafter, the children shall draw lots to determine the order of selection of the various items of tangible personal property; the selection process shall continue in the same order until all of the items have been distributed. Each child shall exchange an appropriate number of chits for each item of personal property selected.

The balance of the Survivor's and Marital Trusts shall be distributed to or for the benefit of such one or more persons and entities, including the estate of the survivor, as the survivor may appoint by Will or a Codicil.

# Personal Financial Statement

## PERSONAL ASSETS OF JACK & GENNY ROYCE

**Current Assets:**

| | |
|---|---|
| Cash in Bank | $6,000 |
| Home Savings | $68,500 |
| Community Bank | $76,000 |
| Great Western S&L | $47,500 |
| 1st National Bank | $2,000 |
| Life Insurance Cash Value | $30,000 |
| Notes Receivables | $90,789 |
| Personal Property | $181,000 |
| Stocks | $70,776 |
| Total Current Assets | $572,565 |

**Fixed Assets:**

| | |
|---|---|
| 100% interest in Royce Supplies Corp | $470,000 |
| Real Estate | |
| 1233 E 23rd Street (Residence) | $300,000 |
| 1235 E 23rd Street | $85,000 |
| Arvin Triplex* | $102,000 |
| Arvin Vacant Lot* | $68,000 |
| Total Fixed Assets | $1,025,000 |

| | |
|---|---|
| **TOTAL ASSETS:** | **$1,597,565** |

**Liabilities:**

| | |
|---|---|
| Mortgage on Residence | $14,000 |

| | |
|---|---|
| **NET WORTH:** | **$1,583,565** |

**Additional:**

| | |
|---|---|
| Life Insurance Death Benefits | $218,000 |

| | |
|---|---|
| **TOTAL ESTATE VALUE:** | **$1,801,565** |

* These assets are the separate property of Genny Royce, all other assets are deemed to be community property. Client supplied information regarding estimated market value of assets, and form of ownership.

# Life Insurance

| Company, Policy #, Type | Face Value, Owner | Premium, Insured | Cash Value, Beneficiary |
|---|---|---|---|
| Prudential 986456499 Whole Life | $100,000 Genny Royce | $6,500 Genny Royce | $85,000 Jack Royce |
| MONY 107478-0SNY Life Payable 28 years | $25,000 Genny Royce | $1,224 Genny Royce | $16,000 Jack Royce |
| MONY 928748-38938 3yrs Mod. Life | $5,000 Genny Royce | $93 Genny Royce | $2,100 Jack Royce |
| MONY B174646-8484 FS Adjustable Life | $50,000 Genny Royce | $3,000 Genny Royce | $12,000 Robert Lansing |
| **GENNY ROYCE TOTAL** | **$180,000** | **$10,817** | **$115,100** |
| Continental Western C00123568 Paid Up | $4,840 Jack Royce | $0 Jack Royce | $2,900 Joint Trust |
| Equitable Combined 3 pol. Life | $23,500 Jack Royce | $0 Jack Royce | $15,750 Joint Trust 1972 |
| NSLJ V1334530-30 Ordinary Life | $5,000 Jack Royce | $95 Jack Royce | $2,550 Joint Trust 1972 |
| NSLJ V 1-34555-56 30 Pay | $5,000 Jack Royce | $102 Jack Royce | $4,600 Joint Trust 1972 |
| **JACK ROYCE TOTAL** | **$38,340** | **$197** | **$25,800** |
| **GRAND TOTAL** | **$218,340** | **$11,014** | **$140,900** |

There are no estate tax consequences upon the death of the first spouse, but there may be additional estate tax consequences upon the death of the second spouse.

# Desired Objectives

## OF JACK & GENNY ROYCE

**Personal:**

- To maintain financial security during your lives.
- To maintain flexibility during your lives.

**Family:**

- To minimize potential family conflicts.
- To treat your heirs fairly upon your demise.

**Business:**

- Have turned over the ownership of the business to your business heirs.
- To pass the business intact to your business heirs.

**Financial:**

- To minimize your estate taxes.
- To minimize administrative costs at death.
- To facilitate gifts to your heirs.

# Objectives Achieved and Not Achieved

## OBJECTIVES ACHIEVED

### Personal:

- You have the means of remaining financially secure during your life.
- Your current estate plan allows you to maintain flexibility.

### Family:

- Your estate plan treats your heirs fairly upon your demise.

### Business:

- You have a way to pass the business intact to your business heirs.

### Financial:

- Your revocable living trust minimizes administrative costs.

## OBJECTIVES NOT ACHIEVED

### Family:

- Your estate plan does not minimize the potential for family conflicts.
- Your estate plan may not treat your heirs fairly upon your demise.

### Business:

- You have not arranged your business affairs so as to be able to eventually turn over the actual operation of your business to your heirs and yet retain financial control during your lifetime.
- It may be difficult to pass the business intact to the business heirs and still treat any non-business heirs fairly at your demise because of the nature of your assets.
- You have not created a business-like approach between family members and the business in order to have the business survive and create harmony within the family.

### Financial:

- Existing wills should be examined by your attorney to make sure you are taking advantage of the recent tax law changes in federal estate tax law.

# Suggestions for Consideration

## MINIMIZE ESTATE SHRINKAGE

### Current Situation: Separate Property

At the death of a spouse, there is no stepped-up basis.

### Consideration: Change to Community Property Ownership

Consider an agreement between you and your spouse that all separate property assets shall become community property, thereby obtaining stepped-up basis. There are considerations other than economic.

## MINIMIZE FAMILY/BUSINESS CONFLICTS

To minimize the conflicts that arise in families, it is important to recognize and acknowledge their cause. The fear of conflict itself is often a source of conflict. The solution to the family member who fears the conflict then is to not disagree openly. Most times these matters can be resolved through the processing of the conflict itself, though it is sometimes useful to do so with a third party present who can ensure that all views are brought up and dealt with.

Often, the origins of these conflicts stem from the interplay of personalities in the early family history. One of the most frequent causes of conflict is lack of effective, honest communication. Business families tend not to take the time to discuss items that are important to all family members. The topics become "shelved" for later, and it seems that later never comes. The result is that these unstated concerns transform themselves into anger and resentment and these are often expressed in ways unrelated to the real concern.

Another cause of conflict is the inability of the family to make a distinction between family life and their business life. While very often this is a blur, it is because the families don't take the time to establish family business purpose and family harmony. Once goals are established, it is important to communicate them to all family members to air and resolve conflicts with other's goals.

When more than one family member is involved in the operation of the business, conflicts can arise over compensation and responsibility, and sometimes commitment. It is not uncommon to hear "I work harder than he does and we get the same pay" from two children. For this reason it is important to spell out responsibilities so that each family member knows exactly what his/her responsibilities are. Furthermore, among family members it is valuable to foster and develop a sense of cooperation.

To increase family harmony and business profitability we recommend you create a more business like approach.

## PASS BUSINESS INTACT TO THE BUSINESS HEIRS

There are several alternatives to be considered, none of which are mutually exclusive. You may consider any or all of them.

### Alternative A: Pass Assets Under a Revocable Living Trust

Benefits to be achieved:

- Allows you to maintain your financial security, as you will be able to continue the business.
- Permits you to maintain control.

Potential problems:

- Fails to minimize estate taxes because: as the value of the business appreciates, much of the increase in value must be used to pay the increased estate taxes.
- May prevent you from treating your children fairly at your deaths unless all of your children wish to be involved in the business.
- Fails to assure your children, even if they should decide to remain and spend years working in the business, that they will be able to inherit it (unless an option to buy the business is agreed upon). You, at any time, could change your trust and disinherit any or all of your children. In addition, economic conditions may be such that the business would have to be sold either before or after your death to discharge unexpected indebtedness or estate shrinkage costs.

### Alternative B: Create A Business Continuation Agreement

Benefits to be achieved:

- Permits you to keep the business intact for the business heirs.
- Permits you to treat your children fairly at your demise.
- Prevents non-family members from maintaining an interest in the property unless other family members agree.
- Allows you to provide for your family's financial security through the funded Business Continuation Agreement.

Potential problems:

- The business heirs would need liquidity to buy out the non-business heirs' interest in the business.

- Any decisions regarding the future ownership of the business become multilateral rather than unilateral.

## CONCLUSIONS

In view of your current family objectives, and business and financial situations, it is recommended that you consider implementing the following:

### Disposition of Your Estate at Death

- You should review your living (revocable) trust (see Glossary: Trusts, Living Trust, Revocable for definition) and determine if all of your assets have been transferred to it in order to pass your property outside probate, thus saving probate costs and enabling you to pass your property quickly and privately.
- Your Wills should be reviewed. They will dispose of your personal effects that are not included in the living trust.
- With regard to property ownership, where husband and wife will retain title to property, you should consider converting any property held separately or in joint tenancy to community property to provide for a stepped-up basis. (Basis may also be stepped down if assets have declined in value between the date of acquisition and the date of death).
- Each of you should review your Durable Power of Attorney in case of injury or disability of either spouse (see GLOSSARY: Power of Attorney, Durable). Re-examine successor appointee.
- Examine your durable Power of Attorney for health care to update your Living Will.
- You should see your attorney for a review and update of your existing legal documents to ensure that your objectives are achieved, and solicit his recommendations for additional "tools" needed.
- Your attorney should examine your present will and trust to determine if they require changes to take advantage of current tax laws.

### Gifting

- To help reduce your taxable estate each of you could take advantage of the Annual Gift Tax Exclusion up to $10,000 per recipient by giving corporate stock, create a limited real estate partnership or give an undivided interest in real estate, or gift life insurance.
- You could also consider making a gift using part of your Unified Tax Credit now which translates into a gift of property worth a maximum of $625,000 per spouse. Such a gift would further reduce your taxable estate to the extent of any post-gift appreciation of the property. For example, if a por-

tion of the estate is taxed in the 50% bracket the estate tax savings could exceed $312,500 per spouse.

- A gift may also be made by using a Wealth Replacement Trust for the benefit of your family. This trust may transfer life insurance on your life to keep the proceeds out of your taxable estate and provide liquidity in the event of your death. However, transfers to a Wealth Replacement Trust will not qualify for the gift tax annual exclusion unless special trustee provisions are added.

## Minimize Potential Family Conflicts

- Execute a written Business Continuation Agreement (see Glossary: Business Continuation Agreement) to assure the uninterrupted continuation of your business within your family without outside interference. Should provide terms for the valuation and purchase of principal's interest in the event of early withdrawal, disability, and/or death (See Alternative B).

- We recommend family discussions regarding the family and how family members may plan for their individual families with a minimum of conflict. The results will create less stress and more harmony for all.

- It is recommended that you have scheduled business meetings to increase trust through communications. You should select a family member on a rotating basis to lead these business meetings. Weekly, monthly, and/or quarterly meetings are recommended.

- It is recommended that you include key non-family employees in your business meetings.

## Liquidity

- At this time, you should review your life insurance policies to determine if the type of contract ownership, and beneficiaries are consistent with your other planning and carry out your objectives.

- The conveyance of assets to the Living Trust and the lifetime gift program can help reduce your overall liquidity needs, and if your estate qualifies for Special Use Valuation (see Post-mortem Considerations) the amount of liquidity needed would be reduced further.

- Provide the necessary liquidity to fund the Business Continuation Agreement including buying out non-business heir's interest in the events of death, disability and retirement and/or pay the estate shrinkage costs and other debts without liquidating or encumbering your current business assets.

# Current Distribution of Assets

## UPON DEATH, BEFORE ESTATE TAXES & ADMINISTRATIVE COSTS

| Heir/Description of Inheritance | | Distribution |
|---|---|---|
| **Sally Royce** | | |
| 1/4 of community property* | | $272,500 |
| Sally Royce Total | | $272,500 |
| **Tom Royce** | | |
| 1/4 of community property* | | $272,500 |
| Tom Royce Total | | $272,500 |
| **Philip Royce** | | |
| 100% Royce Supplies/IPS only | | $470,000 |
| Philip Royce Total | | $470,000 |
| **Wendy Royce** | | |
| 1/4 of community property* | | $272,500 |
| Wendy Royce Total | | $272,500 |
| **Robert Lansing** | | |
| 1/4 of community property* | | $272,500 |
| Beneficiary Genny MONY life policy A877603WS | | $50,000 |
| Triplex Real Estate Arvin, MT, Genny Separate | | $102,000 |
| Robert Lansing Total: | | $424,500 |
| **Vicki Schroeder** | | |
| Duplex & vacant lot, Genny Separate | $88,000 | |
| Vicki Schroeder Total | | $88,000 |
| **TOTAL TAXABLE ESTATE DISTRIBUTION** | | **$1,800,000** |
| Less Unified Credit | | $1,300,000 |
| Estimated Net Taxable Estate | | $500,000 |
| Estimated Federal Estate Taxes | | $250,000 |

* Less Royce Supplies Stock

# Proposed Distribution of Assets

## UPON DEATH, BEFORE ESTATE TAXES & ADMINISTRATIVE COSTS

| Heir/Description of Inheritance | Proposed Distribution |
|---|---|
| **Wendy Royce** | |
| 1/4 of community property* | $256,000 |
| 1/5 of Wealth Replacement Trust** | $43,600 |
| Wendy Royce Total | $299,600 |
| **Sally Royce** | |
| 1/4 of community property* | $256,000 |
| 1/5 of Wealth Replacement Trust** | $43,600 |
| Sally Royce Total | $299,600 |
| **Tom Royce** | |
| 1/4 of community property* | $256,000 |
| 1/5 of Wealth Replacement Trust** | $43,600 |
| Tom Royce Total | $299,600 |
| **Philip Royce** | |
| 50% of Royce Supplies/IPS stock: present gift*** | $235,000 |
| 1/5 of Wealth Replacement Trust** | $43,600 |
| Philip Royce Total | $278,600 |
| **Robert Lansing** | |
| % of community property to equal others* | $154,000 |
| Triplex Real Estate Arvin, MT specific bequest* | $102,000 |
| 1/5 of Wealth Replacement Trust** | $43,600 |
| Robert Lansing Total | $299,600 |
| **Vicki Schroeder** | |
| Duplex & vacant lot: specific bequest* | $88,000 |
| Vicki Schroeder Total | $88,000 |

**TOTAL TAXABLE ESTATE DISTRIBUTION**    **$1,347,000**

Less Unified Credit    $1,065,000
($235,000 used in 1999 stock gift to Philip)

Estimated Net Taxable Estate    $ 282,000
Estimated Federal Estate Taxes#    $141,000

\* Less Royce Supplies Stock and specific bequests to Michael and Vicki

\*\* Wealth Replacement Trust: $218,000 life insurance will not be included in your estate for estate taxes, assuming insured lives three years

\*\*\* Proposal: Phil will presently purchase other 50% of Royce Supplies Stock using private annuity or installment sale

\# Federal Estate taxes will be further reduced or eliminated if you each begin to make use of $10,000 annual exclusion.

# FBR System
# Specialist Training Experience

Following is the schedule for the two-day training seminar for new Wealth Transfer Specialists. This is a two-day classroom-style interactive training event. This training is activity-based and focuses on developing the skills necessary to become an effective Wealth Transfer Specialist.

**At the end of the two days of training, participants will be able to:**

- Conduct interviews of family members for purposes of determining the family's objectives with regard to business succession planning and the transfer of the family's wealth.
- Enter data for a new wealth transfer plan into the FBR Report Generation Software.
- Skillfully present the new wealth transfer plan to family members in a family retreat setting.
- Market themselves as Wealth Transfer Specialists.

**Day One**

- Introduction and Overview of the FBR Model
- Understanding the Current Plan
- Understanding Personality Styles
- Communication Skills
- Case Study Workshop
- Understanding Wealth Transfer Options
- Using the FBR Report Generation Software
- Personality Styles Revisited

**Day Two**

- Organizing the Family Retreat
- Facilitation Tips
- Role-play: The Family Retreat
- Marketing Approaches and Techniques
- The Owner Seminar Presentation
- The Family Seminar Presentation
- Wrap-up and Evaluation

# Expand your practice by using the FBR System[SM] to renew family businesses

## Four ways to obtain additional information about the FBR System:

- Clip and mail the form below to:

  FBR System, Inc.
  P. O. Box 2347
  Avila Beach CA 93424-2347

- Call FBR System, Inc. at 805-595-2089

- Visit www.fbrsystem.com

- e-mail info@fbrsystem.com

---